rock your stars

YOUR ASTROLOGICAL GUIDE TO GETTING IT ALL

HOLIDAY MATHIS

SEAL PRESS

ROCK YOUR STARS
YOUR ASTROLOGICAL GUIDE TO GETTING IT ALL

© 2007 Holiday Mathis

Published by
Seal Press
A Member of the Perseus Books Group
1400 65th Street, Suite 250
Emeryville, CA 94608

9 8 7 6 5 4 3 2 1
Library of Congress Cataloging-in-Publication Data:
Mathis, Holiday.
Rock your stars : your astrological guide to getting it all / Holiday Mathis.
p. cm.
ISBN-13: 978-1-58005-217-7
ISBN-10: 1-58005-217-7
1. Astrology. I. Title.

BF1708.M38 2007
133.5—dc22
2007039235

Cover design by Kimberly Glyder
Interior design by Domini Dragoone
Printed in the United States of America
Distributed by Publishers Group West

Names, places, and identifying details in this book have been changed or obscured by the author to protect the privacy of individuals.

FOR STUART, LEVI, AND
PSYCHIC MAMA JOAN, WHO ROCK.
TOTALLY ROCK. OMNIPOTENTLY ROCK.

★ ARIES ★
MARCH 21–APRIL 19

★ TAURUS ★
APRIL 20–MAY 20

★ GEMINI ★
MAY 21–JUNE 21

★ CANCER ★
JUNE 22–JULY 22

★ LEO ★
JULY 23–AUGUST 22

★ VIRGO ★
AUGUST 23–SEPTEMBER 22

★ LIBRA ★
SEPTEMBER 23–OCTOBER 23

★ SCORPIO ★
OCTOBER 24–NOVEMBER 21

★ SAGITTARIUS ★
NOVEMBER 22–DECEMBER 21

★ CAPRICORN ★
DECEMBER 22–JANUARY 19

★ AQUARIUS ★
JANUARY 20–FEBRUARY 18

★ PISCES ★
FEBRUARY 19–MARCH 20

★ CONTENTS ★

carpe destiny

INTRODUCTION

As an astrologer whose horoscopes appear in newspapers around the world, I often get letters from readers asking me about destiny. *What is it?* they want to know. Is it a fixed thing? If what is going to happen to me is already mapped out, what's the point in trying to do anything to change my life? I might as well kick back on my sofa with a glass of wine and sitcom reruns and wait to see what happens, right? I'm thinking . . . *no.*

Maybe sometimes it seems that way. Sure, it's easy to think that if you had a better destiny, instead of sitting on the sofa with your wineglass and the remote, you'd have supersonic brainpower, major reserves of bravado, a big bank account, clearly defined goals for the future, healthy relationships with everyone you know, and a constant sense of inner peace. You'd have your life all figured out, without even trying.

But that's not the way it works. It may seem like others have better luck or destiny than you, but here's the real truth: *Your stars are only as lucky as you make them.*

Whatever your sign is, and whatever you want out of life, I can assure you that you have wonderful and unique configurations in your astrological chart just waiting to be explored, exploited, and put to the test in your own adventure. If you're ready to *carpe destiny,* to seize your stars and make the most of them, then you can create the fabulous, meaningful, balanced life—full of bank and brains and bravado, not to mention love and friendship and a functional life plan—that you've always dreamed of. As with everything else, it's just a matter of knowing how to work the system—in this case, the astrological system. And I can show you how.

WORKING IT

Using astrology for personal benefit is nothing new. Astrology has been a powerful influence in people's lives since the first cavegirl looked to the heavens, pondering, *Is he really right for me? He seems kinda . . . brutish.*

Early humans tracked the stars to predict the seasons and the weather, to know when to plant, when to harvest, what direction to travel, and when to go. Soon, however, stargazers began to discover what they believed were associations between the movements of the planetary bodies and their own moods, love lives, finances, health, crops, and fertility.

When the moon was full, for instance, it was said to be a time of passion and celebration. And when Venus and the sun were in conjunction, new relationships came into being, opening doors of possibility for friends and lovers.

These ancient people called the associations between what was happening in the skies and what was happening here on earth "omens," and to explain them, they attributed human characteristics to the planets, spinning stories about the planets' lives and their influences on humans' daily actions. Jupiter, for example, was a hedonist and a lord of excess. Sometimes he inspired financial windfalls—other times, hangovers. Venus was a vixen whose stint in the skies could afflict humans with lovesickness and distrust between partners.

People also tuned in to the stars like we tune in to television today—for entertainment. For the Greeks, stargazing was like watching prime-time programming. The gods and goddesses were the actors and actresses, who each night ruled the planets, cast spells on humans, turned each other into constellations, fought, made up, and fought some more. (Think *Desperate Housewives* gone planetary.)

These stories and others eventually intersected and evolved together into the vivid panoply of time-tested beliefs, characteristics, and associations that are the basis of astrology today.

I get thousands of letters from astrology readers, but my favorites are the ones that start, "I don't believe in astrology . . . " and end " . . . so what's in the stars for me?" Plenty of people don't believe, but "believing" is kind of beside the point. You can use astrology whether you're a believer or not. Astrology provides an opportunity to pause for self-reflection. It's all about the personal: What's happening to you, in your life and in your head? Instead of expecting your horoscope to predict the future, try reading your horoscope at the *end* of the day—as a way of looking back on the events and interactions you've had since you woke up, and thinking about what they meant to you, how they shaped you, what your reactions said about you. Sometimes an astrological reading is so spot-on, so revealing, it blows your mind. And you feel a moment of connection when that happens, like you must be on the right path—like the universe is on your side.

Other times, astrology is just plain fun.

Carl Jung, the founder of analytical psychology—and a known student of astrology—believed that the mythical characters in astrology, or "archetypes," sprang from the "collective unconscious," which he believed to be a vast sea of information that all people contribute to and can access. I think that within the collective unconscious is the entirety of everything that has happened, is happening, will happen, and could happen. Jung also wrote that people can access this information in different ways: Some people write down their dreams, some meditate or do yoga, some talk to therapists. Others gaze into a pool of water, a crystal ball, or the bottom of a teacup.

My way is to look up and start a conversation with the stars.

THE NOTORIOUS "D"

And now, readers, what *is* destiny? An excellent question. Let me try to answer it for you.

Destiny isn't just one thing. She takes many forms, and it's your job to spot her when she pops up in your life. She's the cool teacher who, back in the fourth grade, seated you next to your future best friend. She's the fender bender that taught you to be a better driver, so months later, when the other guy ran a red light, you were on the defensive. She's the quiet whisper in your ear that says, *Sign up for belly dancing classes* or, *It's your turn to say you're sorry* or, *Go to Rome!*

And, yes, sometimes destiny speaks to you through a horoscope or through an understanding of planets transiting your astrological chart. Or through a book like this one.

So, what can you do to affect your own destiny? Start by reading this book and learning about the planetary influences that are special to you and your life. Dig in. Engage. Turn these pages. Learn, explore, laugh a little, think a lot about your life and where you're headed—and then get out into the real world that's waiting for you, and hook up with destiny. I understand that it may not always be easy or simple. When you have a date with destiny, sometimes you get stood up. Sometimes it's you who shows up too late. But sometimes everything goes so perfectly, it's almost as if the stars were all aligned in your favor.

I bet they are.

★ solar power

YOUR SUN SIGN

This has happened to you. You go to a party expecting the familiar—the music, the food, the banter, the mixing and mingling—all in a sociable, comfortable groove. But this time, there's a new person at the party, someone asking fun and pointed questions and stirring up the energy. Suddenly, you're seeing a totally different side of your old familiar self. You're spouting witticisms to the crowd, though you usually tend to be laid-back and observant; you're sharing stories you'd forgotten all about, like when you were busted for shoplifting in fourth grade. How is it you never told that one?

Maybe you find yourself jamming out a song on the piano when yesterday you were sure you couldn't remember the difference between an A flat and an arpeggio. Then you leave the party feeling like you're someone a little different from when you walked in. It's still you, but it's a version of you that allows a whole new set of characteristics and perspectives to do the walking and talking.

It's a rare occurrence, but it happens. And it's cool when it does. Breaks you out of the tick-tock, day-to-day ho-hum and makes you see not only yourself, but the world at large, as a place of deeper possibility than you had imagined previously. *What else don't I know about myself?* you wonder. *What other parts of me do I not notice, or forget about, or keep buried under dusty drop cloths in my brain?* And in your wonder, you are glimpsing a spiritual truth: Every person, including you, is a universe of infinite potential.

But wait. Before you get too excited, I must warn: This cosmic "wow, dude" moment is often cut off abruptly by a follow-up spiritual truth: Infinity presents too many potentials to choose from. Like a six-page restaurant menu with long columns of entrées to consider, it's too overwhelming to grapple with the unlimited. That's why so many of us just order "the usual"—it's safe, easy, predictable, and pretty yummy. So where's the bad in that?

No *bad* in it, exactly. But before you know it, you'll be coming to the conclusion many others do when in a similar state of facing down unlimited possibility: *It's so much easier thinking I know who I am than trying to figure out what I could be.* Easier, but so much less fun. And far, far less rewarding.

Now, the classic advice to those seeking to grow or change or find new life paths is to do some good old-fashioned soul-searching; take a long look inward and see what's really there. And I think that's fine advice. Seeing what's inside can be a powerful experience, full of revelation and insight and epiphany.

Except when it isn't.

Sometimes we turn within and all we find are more question marks, diversions, distractions, and fodder for procrastination. If you've ever sat yourself down to ponder a romantic problem, only to find yourself eating nachos over the sink before the second hand has rounded the clock, you know what I mean. And you who once sat down to budget your money or find a new job or plan a vacation and wound up wrapped up in *Days of Our Lives,* you also know what I mean.

Sometimes, when we're just not sure what to do, where to go, what to buy or say or think, or even who to *be,* we have to turn *outward* to get that spark, that idea that can get things moving and grooving and get our problems solved, our lives in gear.

Here's an idea: Let your sun sign be that spark. Just like that groovy new chick at the party who brings out something different in everyone she meets, astrology can be the catalyst that mixes it up, shining the disco ball of life on your lesser-known attributes, attitudes, and talents. Let your stars provide provocative suggestions that can make you look at yourself differently in the mirror and talk differently to yourself in your head, not to mention dress funkier, shop more consciously, or date more open mindedly than you ever thought you would. Because that, dear reader, is the absolute beauty of astrology: *Your stars can help you get to know yourself even better than you already do.*

Take a look at how these fab females used their astro-info to the fullest to take charge of their lives:

LETTA, a Libra just out of college, was stuck about what to do for a career. She led with her sign's natural knack for diplomacy when she volunteered for the Peace Corps. Ultimately, she discovered her calling and now heads a nonprofit agency promoting free trade.

GRETCHEN, forty-three and discouraged by her marital status (or lack thereof), decided to embrace her Aquarian sign's reported proclivity for popularity by throwing a party for every month of the year.

She met her match at one of her fetes—he was a friend of a friend of a friend—and while she's still entertaining every four weeks or so, now her husband helps with the dishes the morning after.

DEBRA, a twenty-six-year-old Virgo and mother of two, had a need for order and organization in her household that led her to design a hanging system for organizing toys. The system is now patent pending, and Debra's not just organized, she's incorporated.

What you notice and identify with about your astrological sign is a tool for self-knowledge. And what you *don't* identify with about your sign is also a tool for self-knowledge, because when you know who you're *not*, then you're closer to knowing who you are.

Now go on—mix and mingle and spend some quality time with you. You're gonna love you, all of you! I'm absolutely sure of it.

ARIES

THE BASICS:

Dates: **March 21–April 19**

Symbol: **ram**

Element: **fire**

Modality: **cardinal**

Yin or yang?: **yang**

Ruler: **Mars**

Body parts: **head and face**

THE ASTRONOMY: The sun glides boldly into Aries with all the confidence of a rock star and twice the bravado—and this transit heralds the vernal equinox. ("Equinox" means a day in which the daytime and nighttime are an equal number of hours.) The vernal equinox is the official beginning of spring (March twenty-first or close to it, depending on the year), in which the sun crosses the celestial equator. But it's also the beginning of the astrological year. Aries embodies the spirit of spring and the celebration of the firstborn child of the zodiac.

THE LEGEND IN A NUTSHELL: There are these twins, Phrixus and Helle, who get into some trouble with an evil stepmother who, in true fairytale fashion, hates their guts and is plotting to kill them. So Zeus sends a ram to rescue them. That turns out to be a kinda dumb idea, even for a god. Helle doesn't make it—she drowns on the journey. But Phrixus gets to safety and then, in tribute to Helle, sacrifices the ram and hangs up the fleece, which turns to gold.

What happens after that is a total dramatic mess involving monsters, battles, a guy named Jason and some Argonauts, grand quests, special effects, and an ending so lame it could bankrupt a Hollywood studio.

Jason endures heroic trials in order to obtain the golden fleece and prove himself to be a super guy, and then messes it all up by cheating on his sorceress wife, who in turn makes him impotent. Roll credits.

But the good part is, the ram—Aries—gets turned into a constellation as a memorial to the whole bloody mishap. Suffice it to say, the Aries legend was forged in the bitter sacrifices of war, but it highlights the heroism that is born of a passionate cause.

ARIES STRENGTHS: your moxie. Your adorable big mouth. Your initiative. Your willingness to make a move when no one else has the guts. Your rebel badness. Your impulsive correctness. The quiet stands you take on a daily basis that wind up yelling out who you are. Your integrity.

ARIES WEAKNESSES: your temper. Your jealousy. Your tendency to rescue people who would be better off saving themselves. Your temper. Oh yeah, and your temper.

ARIES SUPERPOWER: beginner's luck. Every endeavor has an inherent risk. The beauty of an Aries is that she hasn't learned what that risk is, so she is able to act wholeheartedly and is ultimately willing to risk it all. Aries' cosmic energy zings with freshness, newness, *now*-ness, and she embodies the paradox of the beginner: When you've got nothing, you've got nothing to lose. Our experiences in life teach us when to be fearful, but when we have no experience to draw from—when it's our first kiss, our first time on a tennis court, our first day on the job—we haven't learned our limitations yet. So the outcome is often better than one born of years of practice.

CRISIS CONTROL IN ARIESLAND:

1. Choose a goal.
2. Dive into it with your whole heart, oblivious to the risk.
3. Everything will change.

ARIES MANTRA: *I rule. Omnipotently. Get out of my way.*

★ TAURUS ★

THE BASICS:

Dates: **April 20–May 20**

Symbol: **bull**

Element: **earth**

Modality: **fixed**

Yin or yang?: **yin**

Ruler: **Venus**

Body parts: **ears, neck, and throat**

THE ASTRONOMY: Taurus is the middle sign of the spring season. If we could turn back the clocks to about 4000 BC, the sun's position on the vernal equinox—the date when day and night are the exact same length, which happens to be the beginning of the astrological year and the first day of spring—would actually be in Taurus, not Aries, as it is now. Therefore, early civilizations actually considered Taurus the first constellation of the zodiac. (You see, we are drifting through the universe, and so our point of view changes to the tune of one degree every 71.6 years—a slow, but cumulative, effect.) So one millennium, after their perspectives underwent this slight shift, humans realized, "Oh, wow. I think Aries is actually first."

This reminds me of when my friend Darcy found out that her dad had had a son with a different woman before she was born. What all this means is that Taurus has all the conviction of a firstborn child, mixed with the gracious humility that comes from finding out that she isn't actually first.

THE LEGEND IN A NUTSHELL: Taurus is a god disguised as a cow. Greek gods are notoriously sneaky, especially when they fall in love (or, ahem, lust). In the case of Taurus, Zeus becomes smitten with a human princess, Europa, and somehow decides that his best come-on would be to turn himself into a gorgeous bovine. (While this doesn't make much sense to anyone living in a fast-food nation, there are cultures that worship, or at least admire, animals that say "moo," and they might have more insight into why the ploy actually worked.) Europa rode that crazy white bull clear across the sea, and when they got to the island of Crete, Zeus did a big reveal. And Europa was like, "Oh, great. You're a god? Where's that hot cow?"

TAURUS STRENGTHS: The Energizer bunny has nothing on you. Just when you think you've had enough of life's knocks, your reserve forces kick in and you can go another round. Your incredible endurance and heart turn ordinary circumstances into winning dramas of cinematic scope. Also, you're stable, trustworthy, composed, magnetic, and doggone funny. Oh yeah, and you have a really cool voice.

TAURUS WEAKNESSES: It's so wonderful that you never give up. Except sometimes you should. When it's not working, that can be a sign to change your approach—a sign you miss easily. Don't be stubborn. Listening to the advice of loved ones can keep you from falling into a tragic rut.

TAURUS SUPERPOWER: singing. Your sign rules the throat, and your voice has mystical powers. Now, you don't have to actually be able to sing to be a singer. Confused? Don't think Alicia Keys, think animals in the forest—a primal expression of breath and intention.

CRISIS CONTROL IN TAURUSLAND:

1. Take a deep breath.

2. **Allow your throat to hold on to it,** wrap around it, massage and mold it, caress and carve it, as you freely . . .

3. **Let it out.** The universe will harmonize. What's broken gets fixed, what's missing gets found, what's needed falls into your hand.

TAURUS MANTRA: *I have all I need. And what I don't have, I can buy online and have overnighted to me by FedEx.*

 ★ GEMINI ★

THE BASICS:

Dates: **May 21–June 21**

Symbol: **twins**

Element: **air**

Modality: **mutable**

Yin or yang?: **yang**

Ruler: **Mercury**

Body parts: **nervous system, shoulders, arms, lungs, and rib cage**

THE ASTRONOMY: Since the constellation looks like two parallel stick figures, it's easy to see how the twins theme caught on. People can connect the star dots in different ways, and it still comes out looking like twins. One twin appears to be in the Milky Way, and the other isn't—which creates all kinds of intrigue. Maybe one is naughty and one is nice. Maybe one has been locked out of the Milky Way galaxy for bad behavior, and the other one is regaling his fellow stars about the deliciously dastardly deeds done by his evil twin.

THE LEGEND IN A NUTSHELL: Like I said, Geminis are twins. Sort of. Like Castor and Pollux of the Gemini legend, who share the same mother but have two different fathers. One was fathered by a swan (that is to say, Zeus doing another one of his pervy bestial impersonations), and the other was fathered by a mortal king. And the twins love each other. They are very successful and popular (think Mary-Kate and Ashley Olsen, only with penises and without rehab). Side by side they date women, fight the Trojan War, and get rich and famous . . . until one horrible day when Castor dies. Pollux is so overwrought with grief over the knowledge that he's doomed to live eternally without his bitchin' other half that his god-father takes pity on him and changes all the rules. He tosses the two of them up into the heavens, where they remain immortally connected.

GEMINI STRENGTHS: your wit. You're born to communicate and you do it with style. You come up with the kind of zingers that make people do spit-takes. When you like someone, your compliments are more valuable than gifts from Tiffany, all bowed up. And it's so savvy how you can breeze through an insult and make it sound, to the untrained ear, like a compliment.

GEMINI WEAKNESSES: There's a time to talk and a time to shut up. You easily miss the latter. Subtle cues are lost on you. You must work extra hard to listen. You can also be two-faced and gossipy. But, hey, all in the name of good clean fun, right?

GEMINI SUPERPOWER: trendsetting. You have an extra sense about what's hip, happening, and Hot. You realize that there is no one way to be Hot. The very essence of Hot is that it's of the moment, and when the moment passes, Hot turns to Not . . . or, if Hot is lucky, it becomes Cool. But you're not hanging on to Hot long enough for that. You know when to let go and be on to the next Hot thing.

CRISIS CONTROL IN GEMINILAND: When you don't know what to do, learn one thing. About anything. This opens your mind. Before you know it, "anything" leads to "a lot of things," and "a lot of things" includes the one thing you need to know in order to move closer to your destiny.

GEMINI MANTRA: *I can talk my way into anything my heart desires—or out of anything that's a pain in my ass.*

★ ASTROLOGICAL QUESTION ★

"What is a 'Saturn return'? I'm about to turn twenty-nine, and I've heard it's going to be the hardest year of my life. What should I expect?"

You can relax. Despite its bad rep, Saturn return is nothing to be afraid of. "Saturn return" is when Saturn, the planet of lessons, comes back to the place it was when you were born, approximately twenty-nine years after you were born.

Think of it as a kind of graduation: Remember the final days of summer before high school? Rumors spread about how hard things were about to get (what *is* trigonometry, anyway?). Well, Saturn returns seem to have a similar power to instill fear in the minds and hearts of the astrologically inclined. But Saturn, like high school, is simply meant to bring about new levels of maturity and unforgettable experiences.

Now, so maybe it won't be a cakewalk. There will be some stretching and growing you can expect to have to work at as you gain new wisdom. But you'll do great. In fact, enjoy it, and make the most of a rare opportunity to learn everything you can. And by the way, happy birthday.

★ CANCER ★

THE BASICS:

Dates: **June 22–July 22**

Symbol: **crab**

Element: **water**

Modality: **cardinal**

Yin or yang?: **yin**

Ruler: **moon**

Body parts: **breasts, chest, and stomach**

THE ASTRONOMY: The summer solstice (a Latin-derived word meaning "sun stand still") is marked by the sun's annual entrance into Cancer. The summer solstice has been celebrated in one way or another by almost every culture throughout history. June celebrations called Vestalia, the Feast of St. John the Baptist, midsummer, and so on all occur somewhere around the longest day of the year. It's a time when the snow has melted, the ground has thawed, and things are blooming.

THE LEGEND IN A NUTSHELL: Zeus has an affair (big surprise), the result of which is the strapping Greek and Roman favorite, Hercules. Hera, Zeus's wife, wants to kill this love child, but try as she may, the dude is simply too strong. So Hera sits back and waits until the day when Hercules, a risk taker, a daredevil, a macho man, gets into dangerous trouble on his own. Bingo—Hercules soon gets into a fight with a water serpent. Hera sends Cancer, her faithful, valiant little house pet, to aid the water serpent. What was she thinking? Though Cancer may have made a wonderful domestic companion (although one can only imagine the challenges involved in potty-training a crab), she isn't such a great guard-crab. As the poor crustacean is nipping at Hercules' feet, she gets trampled in the scuffle. Hera, accepting defeat for the time being, places the crab's image in the night sky as a reward for her service.

To understand this story's significance, we have to look at it from the crab's point of view. What an honor for a simple crustacean to be asked to fight for a goddess! And though she was ultimately no match for Hercules, she was immortalized for her ferocious sensitivity to the wounded feelings of her mistress.

CANCER STRENGTHS: your intuition. Your magnificent maternal instinct. Your power to nurture and heal without saying a word. The domestic magic you weave. The kick-ass parties you throw. Your devoted patriotism. Your ability to transform a structure into a home.

CANCER WEAKNESSES: You're astute, tuned in, acutely sensitive. However, sometimes the one you are most sensitive toward is yourself. Letting your emotions make or break not only your day, but that of anyone around you, is simply too much power to hand over to a feeling. Use your feelings, but don't let them use you.

CANCER SUPERPOWER: mothering. You don't have to be a mother to be mothering. Your nurturing goes beyond familial ties, beyond friendship—you could be a mother to a total stranger in their hour of need. This is how you heal the world.

CRISIS CONTROL IN CANCERLAND:

1. Go home.
2. Straighten, fluff, cook, polish, inhabit.
3. Invite someone else to join you.

The world suddenly seems custom designed for your comfort. Your company relaxes into you.

CANCER MANTRA: *I feel, therefore I create—magnificently. Also, if I'm not feelin' it, I'm not doin' it, which saves me a lot of trouble.*

THE BASICS:

Dates: **July 23–August 22**

Symbol: **lion**

Element: **fire**

Modality: **fixed**

Yin or yang?: **yang**

Ruler: **sun**

Body parts: **heart, back, and shoulders**

THE ASTRONOMY: The annual solar transit through Leo celebrates the Sun King's return to his throne. Leo is the fifth zodiac constellation and the one most easily recognized: the crouching lion facing westward, with a distinctive head and mane marked by a sickle of stars that looks like a backward question mark.

THE LEGEND IN A NUTSHELL: The lion has symbolized royalty, divinity, and power since ancient times—perhaps because the lion has no natural predators, save man. And, I guess, god, because it was the lion that decided to battle the son of Zeus, Hercules, who is legendarily immortalized in the constellation Leo. Hercules kicks the lion's ass and proceeds to make a costume out of his head and hide—which speaks to the theatrical lineage of the sign. The message seems to be, when you're defeated, grab a costume (or become one, as the case may be) and put on a show! Who knows, maybe your defeat is actually your glory.

LEO STRENGTHS: your playfulness. Your ability to relate to all ages with childlike wonder. Your creativity. Your propensity to delight and entertain others. The passionate way you pretend. Through pretending and imagination, you make it so.

LEO WEAKNESSES: your ego. I could remind you that the world doesn't revolve around you, but I would be lying. Because it's true that everyone's world revolves around them, especially yours. However, you are much more attractive when you at least make believe this isn't the case for long enough to listen to what the other person you're in a conversation with is trying to tell you.

LEO SUPERPOWER: generosity. It's so easy for you to give. You would gladly give away everything—mainly because it would save you from having to organize it. But the weird thing about giving is that it always attracts more. The more you give, the more you have, and the more boxes and closet fixtures you need.

CRISIS CONTROL IN LEOLAND: Get a camera and take a picture of yourself. (Note: This is evidence of your proud existence.) With the detachment of a film director, tell yourself what scene to play out next.

LEO MANTRA: *I'm the star of my life. I model it, and I become it. I act it out, and it is. I should get an Oscar.*

★  ★

THE BASICS:

Dates: **August 23–September 22**

Symbol: **maiden**

Element: **earth**

Modality: **mutable**

Yin or yang?: **yin**

Ruler: **Mercury**

Body part: **digestive system**

THE ASTRONOMY: Because the Virgo solar transit coincides with the harvesting of crops, the constellation is associated with getting things done. Efficiency. Improvement. Health. History has depicted this woman in various ways—sometimes as a demanding goddess, sometimes as an innocent and proper maiden, but usually as one who brings the grains of the harvest for all to enjoy.

THE LEGEND IN A NUTSHELL: Do you remember the tale of Pandora's box? The story begins in an idyllic setting, when the world was Eden-esque. That is to say, nobody ever has to grapple with computerized operators or technical assistance, lines at the grocery store are never more than two people deep, and there are enough parking spaces for all of humanity to be at the mall at the same time. Then along comes Pandora, the first woman, the original Virgo, the pure virgin. She sees that there's this box that has never been opened, and damn it all if she can't find out what might be inside. Rumor has it that she worried it might be in need of deep dusting, or that the inside corners could be harboring toxic mold and could therefore use a little airing out. Whatever her reason, she does the unthinkable—she opens the box.

What happens next is either a nightmare or a wild and wonderful dream, depending on whom you ask. Sin and cynicism are let loose upon the world. Oh, and evil. (These things had reportedly been stuffed into the box by Jupiter during a particularly extensive cleaning spree.) Some rue this innocence lost, while others celebrate it. Without it, there would be no wicked wit, no drama, and nothing "cool," since "cool" (as only the coolest know) relies on a marriage of dark and bright energies. But what is Virgo's role in all of this? Well, maybe somewhere deep inside, she realizes that since she let it all out of the box, it's on her to organize it.

VIRGO STRENGTHS: Organization is the stuff of life—it's the gorgeous efficiency of nature, the structure of DNA, the systematic evolution of the planet.

It's also a fantabulous sock drawer. And no one can organize like you can. Not only are you thoughtful, but you execute plans quickly, seriously, and with great sensitivity. Bosses love you like a wife, especially the women.

VIRGO WEAKNESSES: You sometimes can't resist playing your advantage. Like, the Virgo giveth and so shall she taketh away. You seldom receive the credit due to you, so you feel justified in getting all you can out of a situation. However, if you ever misstep in your attempt to even the score, your relentless guilty conscience is a severe punisher.

VIRGO SUPERPOWER: your purity. Okay, so you're not pure in a driven-snow way, or in a nun way, either. But you are pure in your intent to make the world a more beautiful, clean, and decent place. And when you apply yourself to an improvement, your pure intent helps things get done quickly.

CRISIS CONTROL IN VIRGOLAND:

1. **Decide what needs an upgrade,** and what is needed to create the improvement.
2. **Make lists,** cross things off, make more lists, cross more things off.
3. **Stand back and admire** the fruits of your own magical sweat.

VIRGO MANTRA: *Through expert analysis, I can figure out any problem, sort out any situation, make anything happen. Einstein has nothing on me.*

★ LIBRA ★

THE BASICS:

Dates: **September 23–October 23**

Symbol: **scales**

Element: **air**

Modality: **cardinal**

Yin or yang? **yang**

Ruler: **Venus**

Body parts: **lower back and pelvis, kidneys, ovaries**

THE ASTRONOMY: Libra's solar reign begins on the autumnal equinox. The astronomical occurrence has been celebrated in some form by countless cultures, often with some kind of harvest theme.

THE LEGEND IN A NUTSHELL: In many an astrological myth, the Greeks and Romans elaborated on legends spun by cultures even more ancient than they were. In the case of Libra, the most compelling myth comes from Egypt, and the main player is a dog-headed immortal called Anubis. One of his jobs is to process the red-tape details of death that tend to get tangled up with the transition from here to eternity. And the main tool Anubis puts to the task is a giant scale. Apparently our earthly deeds weigh on the old soul and can be evaluated to determine what humans have coming

★ ASTROLOGICAL QUESTION ★

"I'm a Libra, and I've always been indecisive when it comes to events in my life, whether it's as serious as choosing a career or as insignificant as what to eat for dinner. Will I always be so bad at making decisions?"

You know how to make decisions—really, you do. Weighing the options on the scale of your sign is just a part of your decision-making process. What is frustrating is when you don't even come to a conclusion. You obsess over the what-ifs of a choice until you cry uncle and take the path of least resistance.

Life is an experiment. No one ever really knows how a choice will turn out; they just get adept at playing their odds. And the only way to that is by building experiences—choosing and then choosing again. In time you understand the consequences of your decisions because you live with them. Maybe you will always be indecisive about some things in life. But other things you'll be dead-on sure about in an instant. So trust your own process. Know that your choices, and even your choices not to choose, are all perfect, leading to the exact experiences necessary for you to live to your highest potential.

to them in the afterlife. Though the scales are the only inanimate object of the zodiac, this is not to say they symbolize any less emotional impact than the other symbols. Any woman who's ever gotten down to her goal weight can attest to the sheer elation that scales can generate.

LIBRA STRENGTHS: your eye for art, design, and style. Your taste is impeccable, and part of what makes it so is your ability to meld disparate cultures and time periods. You're a unifying force, partly because of your diplomacy. You're clever, buoyant, and loving—oh yes, loving! Adoring! You love love, even when it hurts. And you risk all for what you love.

LIBRA WEAKNESSES: indecision. Just because you can sit on a fence doesn't make it a chair. And though straddling the middle ground between here and there can be effective in some situations, it's annoying in others. This is something you find out when someone comes along to rattle you and see which side you'll fall down on.

LIBRA SUPERPOWER: egalitarianism. No one is better or worse than anyone else in your book, and you're therefore able to extend compassion that transcends categories. You'd give the same hug to a family member as you would to a visiting alien from the planet Zortor (provided the Zortorian, or the family member, didn't get your outfit gooey—you do hate messing up your clothes).

CRISIS CONTROL IN LIBRALAND:

1. State what you love.

2. **Then state what else you love,** and state more that you love.

3. **Now pour your heart into what you love**—magically, you are even more full than when you started.

LIBRA MANTRA: *I have everything I need to create perfect balance in myself and in my world. Really, really I do. I complete me.*

 **★SCORPIO★**

THE BASICS:

Dates: **October 24–November 21**

Symbol: **scorpion**

Element: **water**

Modality: **fixed**

Yin or yang?: **yin**

Ruler: **Pluto**

Body parts: **reproductive and procreative organs**

THE ASTRONOMY: The Scorpio solar transit is a time of barren trees; browns and golds; dried, withered flowers; and, well, death. It's no coincidence that Halloween falls during the time when the sun is transiting through Scorpio. And it's not the only holiday related to death that occurs at this time of year. The Mexican Day of the Dead and the pagan Samhain, for instance, are two holidays with a similar intent—to honor the spirits and acknowledge the mysterious circle of life.

In the BC era, the constellation Scorpio included several stars that are now designated as part of Libra, which made it the largest constellation at that time. As civilizations evolved and changed, that region of sky was observed differently, and new pictures emerged on the heavenly canvas. The changes that Scorpio has been through, and its many associated symbols, are representative of this sign's energy—the energy of transformation.

THE LEGEND IN A NUTSHELL: Scorpio is a scorpion. And an eagle. And a phoenix. Really.

Why do other astrologers and I attribute numerous symbols to Scorpio? It's a complex and often misunderstood energy. One symbol just doesn't do it justice. And though the scorpion is certainly the most known symbol (a scorpion killed a giant hunter named Orion, but, in keeping with the secretive nature of the sign, the details of this legend seem to be lost in antiquity), I think the legend that most closely mirrors what Scorpio is about is the phoenix.

The phoenix is a mythological creature, some version of which appears in a variety of cultural legends, including Russian, Native American, Chinese, Japanese, and Harry Potter–ese. She's a fantastic bird, all pimped out with fluffy neon plumage and a phat attitude—perhaps because she knows she's immortal. Pretty much. Actually, she does die (according to some, about once every millennium) via spontaneous combustion. But three days later, she rises from her ashes. The message is one for the ages: No matter how fabulous, beloved, and beautiful one is, in order to remain relevant, one must reinvent oneself every so often.

SCORPIO STRENGTHS: your fearlessness. Your intensity. Your willingness to look deeply, searchingly, into the eyes of your problem until the answer emerges. Your eloquence. And your sex appeal, which is innate, effortless, and overwhelming. Do be careful where you fling that!

SCORPIO WEAKNESSES: Sarcasm is one of your favorite coping mechanisms. Okay, you're funny, but there's no long-term benefit to remaining callous. Also, diva-esque vindictiveness may be a terrific quality in soap opera villains, but in real life it's just scary.

SCORPIO SUPERPOWER: mysticism. You often appear to others to have one foot in the spiritual realm. Perhaps you don't believe you are presently involved in a dialogue with the divine, but others believe you are. And that otherworldly quality gives you a powerful presence. When you learn how to use it, you're downright dangerous!

CRISIS CONTROL IN SCORPIOLAND: What do you think your great-great-grandmother would tell you now if she could? Sit quietly and listen, and she'll let you know. Honoring the spirits in this way reminds you that you are a spirit as well—you just happen to be living in the physical world, occupying a body, clothes, and home, while the disembodied spirits are busy walking through walls.

SCORPIO MANTRA: *My passion is the power that can mold the world to my liking. Desire, and a smokin' hot wardrobe, will make it so.*

★ SAGITTARIUS ★

THE BASICS:

Dates: **November 22–December 21**

Symbol: **archer**

Element: **fire**

Modality: **mutable**

Yin or yang?: **yang**

Ruler: **Jupiter**

Body part: **the sciatic nerve, which runs down the hips and legs**

THE ASTRONOMY: Astronomers agree that the constellation Sagittarius is a thrilling visual, whether through a telescope or the naked eye. It's situated on some prime galactic real estate, in what appears to earthlings to be the center of the galaxy. Plus, it includes some young, hot stars and a popular black hole.

THE LEGEND IN A NUTSHELL: Sagittarius is a centaur—half man, half horse. The centaur race happened as a trick of the gods. The creature is descended from Ixion, a mere mortal who has designs on Hera, the wife of the god Zeus. Zeus sends a cloud in the shape of his wife to fool Ixion— oh, how funny! Ixion has sex with the cloud!

This gives Zeus quite a belly laugh, but it isn't so hilarious according to the offspring of their tryst, a weird-looking cloud-guy. What a hellish adolescence poor Cloudy has. Unlike the other clouds, rejected by the gods, and ignored by the people, he's probably not about to find anyone to sit next to in the cafeteria. What's a freaky cloud guy to do? What any freaky cloud guy would do, of course—date a horse!

And thus begins the race of centaurs. They're actually really cool—a melding of magic and hedonism, worldliness and otherworldliness. Sagittarius is one of these centaurs—a fierce fighter whose bow and arrow are always drawn, ready to go off at a moment's provocation.

Sagittarian astral energy contains many elements of this myth. Just as Ixion jealously desired the wife of a god, Sagittarius people are frequently watching what the rest of the world is doing, just to make sure they are not missing out on anything. Also, the idea of an amalgam of influences forming one fierce and magnificent creature still applies. Sagittarians are sophisticated, with global consciousness and great curiosity and tolerance for others very unlike themselves.

SAGITTARIUS STRENGTHS: You're just plain lucky. And you don't hoard that luck, either—you let it rub off on anyone you're currently brushing against. And your adventurous spirit makes sure that you whoosh by a rainbow's array of fascinating characters, not to mention the cherished few you collect for keeps along your glittering path. Your willingness to learn from these influences makes you an unforgettable character your-self, richly diverse, sophisticated, and glamorous.

SAGITTARIUS WEAKNESSES: Those who say you are sincere may be right. But what they don't know is that you just couldn't be bothered to think up a kind lie. Your momentum throughout life sometimes leaves piles of hurt feelings in its wake. And those you think are trapping you are often only trying to get close to you.

SAGITTARIUS SUPERPOWER: tolerance. World peace would absolutely be possible if everyone were as welcoming and open-minded as you. What you realize is that when you extend acceptance to someone else, you are really accepting yourself. As the old song goes, "Let there be peace on earth, and let it begin with me. . . . "

CRISIS CONTROL IN SAGITTARIUSLAND: Go outside. If your next move would usually be to turn right, then turn left. If your next move would usually be to turn left, then turn right. Continue in this manner at every juncture, going the opposite direction of your most known path. Notice how the sky is a slightly different color where you are, the scenery is vivid in its newness, and your thoughts come through with fresh alacrity. Life is, once again, an adventure.

SAGITTARIUS MANTRA: *My mind expands with each added experience and every relationship I forge. Moment by moment, person by person, I will someday understand the entirety of this crazy universe.*

★ CAPRICORN ★

THE BASICS:

Time: **December 22–January 19**
Symbol: **the sea goat**
Element: **earth**
Modality: **cardinal**
Yin or Yang?: **yin**
Ruler: **Saturn**
Body Parts: **knees and skin**

THE ASTRONOMY: The constellation of Capricorn is not so easy to see. Like a stellar VIP, it doesn't need to burn bright in order to project its importance. Its confidence is quiet, its power is more spectacularly felt, not seen. Its most notable luminary is actually a cluster of five stars called "the Algedi," thirty-nine light-years away.

THE LEGEND IN A NUTSHELL: The Capricorn energy is often misunderstood, and it's no wonder. Even its symbol is so strange that it is now commonly simplified into a goat. But it's not just a goat. It's a goat that swims. And it not only swims, it has a tail like a fish, like a mermaid, but it's a goatmaid. Though the sea goat doesn't rate in the mythological popularity contest these days (dragons, faeries and gargoyles being among the current mythological glitterati), images of fishtailed underwater goats have been found in Babylonian tablets over 3,000 years old, suggesting that the sea-goat was once a big player on the mythological circuit. The story goes that the goat-god Pan was trying to escape a monster by way of diving into the sea, so part of his body became a fish. Capricorn was once considered a water sign, but the water theme throughout Capricorn lore has been toned down to fit Capricorn's modern earth sign qualities. The important part to remember is that Capricorn energy is about doing what it takes to get where you need to go, whether that means working late, training hard, or changing your tail into a fishtail to escape a monster.

CAPRICORN STRENGTHS: Your word is gold. It appears that this is true because you're admirably ethical. But really it's because you instinctively understand that the person who claims and upholds responsibility for a situation is the one with the power. And you like having power. In fact, it's kinda your thing. So you are accountable, trustworthy, persevering, untiring, and driven to be the best.

CAPRICORN WEAKNESSES: Accepting where you are can be difficult for you. You're so used to striving to be at the top of your game that you often neglect to acknowledge where you are right now. Don't let ambition rob you of precious moments.

CAPRICORN'S SUPERPOWER: Honoring tradition. Your sentimental heart embraces the importance of ritual and roots. Whether it's celebrating a holiday, paying tribute to a loved one going through a life passage such as a baptism or important birthday, or simply having a nice family dinner, you create ceremonies that perfectly capture the intention of the moment.

CRISIS CONTROL IN CAPRICORNLAND:

1. Pick an impossible task.

2. Attach it to a ridiculously limited time frame.

3. Go for it.

CAPRICORN MANTRA: *I can and will do anything and everything I put my mind to doing, and with such finesse that it will hardly seem like I am working.*

★AQUARIUS★

THE BASICS:

Time: **January 20-February 18**

Symbol: **the waterbearer**

Element: **air**

Modality: **fixed**

Yin or Yang?: **yang**

Ruler: **Uranus**

Body Parts: **the calves, shins, and ankles**

THE ASTRONOMY: Aquarius is one of the oldest noted constellations. Thousands of years ago, the part of sky in which Aquarius shines was known as "The Sea," and the constellations in this part of the sky, including Capricorn (a sea goat) and Pisces (a fish), relate to water. Admittedly, it takes a lot of imagination to link together the image of a person carrying water out of the mostly dim stars that make up the Aquarian constellation. Then again, imagination is what the Aquarius energy is all about.

THE LEGEND IN A NUTSHELL: Aquarius is the sign of the water bearer. In a civilized place where relatively clean water comes out of the taps or can be bought in a bottle at the local convenience store for a dollar, we tend to take H_2O for granted. That is, until something catastrophic happens to remind us how fragile humankind really is. We can live without food for over a month, but without clean water we can be gonners in under 100 hours. These insights are key to understanding the Aquarius energy, which is to generously bring what is needed to the party. This friendly energy has less to do with social nicety and popularity than it does to do with the fact that humans need one another. Without contact, just like without water, they perish.

AQUARIUS STRENGTHS: Your instinct to preserve humanity may be basic, but it presents itself in ways that are anything but. You're innovative, exceptional, eccentric, and gloriously whimsical. You're multi-dimensional, scientific, and endearingly quirky. You dip generously and often into the collective unconscious for inspiration and support, and it always provides you with both. Sometimes it even offers up bits of genius to use however you see fit.

AQUARIUS WEAKNESSES: You find it hard to establish social boundaries. You'd prefer to think that "It's all good, it's all love" but sometimes it's not all good, neither is it even mostly good, and the love part remains to be demonstrated. Once in a while, demand proof of love. If for no other reason than to verify that it really exists.

AQUARIUS SUPERPOWER: Vision. You are tomorrow's child, part sci-fi action heroine, part 21st–century realist. While you're taking the freeway to work, you imagine yourself in a hovercraft—you will ride that vehicle one day. And while you enjoy a first date with a qualified candidate for life-partner, you imagine your immanent domestic bliss—yes, it's as good as done. It may take a decade or two, but your visions do come true.

CRISIS CONTROL IN AQUARIUSLAND: Believe. When it seems foolish to do so. When nobody else will. When you're mocked. When you're praised. Believe. When all indication points to the one fact: Your vision will never be realized. What do they know? Fodder for your desire. All the more reason to believe.

AQUARIUS MANTRA: *I do what's needed to help humanity thrive, best accomplished by helping myself thrive. It's so beautiful when purposes compound!*

★ PISCES ★

THE BASICS:

Dates: **February 19–March 20**
Symbol: **fish**
Element: **water**
Modality: **mutable**

Yin or yang?: **yin**

Ruler: **Neptune**

Body parts: **feet, toes, and lymphatic system**

THE ASTRONOMY: Pisces is not terrifically easy to spot in the sky, but humans as far back as the ancient Syrians have nonetheless been doing so. The constellation resembles two circles connected by a string.

THE LEGEND IN A NUTSHELL: Pisces is two fish, swimming in opposite directions. According to Greek myth, one day the goddess Aphrodite and her son Eros are walking along a riverbank when they run into a monstrous god called Typhon, who is in a pissed-off mood. In fact, he's spitting fire. So they get out of his way. They dive into the river, where they take the form of fish. And because they don't want to lose track of each other, they each hold on to the end of a silver cord. They are now immortalized as the Northern Fish and the Western Fish of Pisces.

The symbol of fish has been used in countless cultures as an icon of salvation, and astrology incorporates this association as well. The fish offer deliverance, recovery, and healing—but this offering doesn't come for free. Just as Aphrodite and Eros had to plunge into the river to save themselves, the promise of Pisces comes with the caveat that we must take the initiative to dive into the sea of our emotions to find our salvation. The stars invite us to react to the monsters and evils of the world by going

★ SHE'S A 𝔓ISCES ★

ERYKAH BADU may be a neo–soul singer, but her soul is ancient indeed—that's a given for Pisces, the sage of the zodiac. Pisces is the sign of spirit, poetry, and music, which Erykah Badu weaves together into a single artistic expression. Her style has been called bohemian hip-hop, R&B, jazz. . . . But she's not quick to classify, claiming that there are "billions of particles of atomic memory of different things" in her music. As the last sign of the zodiac, she is a blend-master, a culmination of all signs before her, able to empathize and harmonize through life because of her unique understanding. Little fishes should take this advice from Ms. Badu: "No matter what is going on in your life, sisters, take your bubble bath." Spoken like a true water sign.

into ourselves to examine our part in that evil. By facing the shadows of such monsters in ourselves, we can escape any peril that can be caused by the outside world. Deep stuff, yeah. Which is why Pisces is the deepest sign of the zodiac.

PISCES STRENGTHS: You are the amalgam of every sign in the zodiac. You represent the fusion of every sign in the zodiac, and your strengths are accordingly multifaceted. You are wise and talented, soulful and sophisticated, sweet and salty. You have your finger on the open wound of humanity, ready to stop the bleeding. You are the Jedi master, the sensei with sex appeal, the phantasmagorical female.

PISCES WEAKNESSES: You need a bodyguard more than any other sign does. But even that wouldn't do. Because what you really need is a soulguard. As a result of your psychic sensitivity, you are impressionable. Being open means being vulnerable to negative influences as well as positive ones.

PISCES SUPERPOWER: mutation. Not as scary as it sounds. Your sign represents the return to the primordial sea bath from which all life evolved, and where all boundaries are dissolved by salt crystals. Your knack for trying on different personalities, physicalities, and points of view is supernatural without being freaky.

CRISIS CONTROL IN PISCESLAND:

1. Dream of who you want to be.
2. Flesh it out mentally in vivid detail, so real that you could practically pluck a molecule from the dream person and, like some kind of futuristic scientist, grow a person from the DNA of that molecule.
3. Pluck a molecule from the dream person and grow your new self from the DNA of that molecule.

PISCES MANTRA: *I believe in my dreams, which are more real than reality. Because of my belief, I can paint with my mind, sing with my soul, and meditate the crap out of anything that's in my way.*

yin my yang

LOVE AND RELATIONSHIPS

The day I met my husband, the skies weren't particularly notable for me. Yes, there was a new Taurus
moon that night—Taurus is a sensual energy, known
for stimulating the senses in general, and the sense of
taste in particular. Typically, under a Taurus moon I'm
very hungry. For chocolate. And dishes I have no idea
how to prepare at home. So when I walked through
the back door of a Los Angeles dinner club that night,
it was more about discovering the romance of soufflé
than the romance of, well, romance. But before I could
say "dessert menu," in walked this guy.

He was angular and tall, with glossy dark eyes that made him seem animated, though he stood quietly among the friends he had come with. I was alone—a rare occurrence since, during my entire twenties, I seemed to always be accompanied by at least one girlfriend. I'm a Leo, hopelessly social at all times, except when it really matters. That night, it mattered.

He noticed me watching him, and without an awkward moment or hesitation, he nodded hi. It wasn't a "Hi, nice to meet you" kind of hi. It was more like, "Hey, it's you!" as if we knew each other already but he wasn't expecting to see me there. Then I realized he was making his way over to me, and that's when my sense of time went quantum—the next ten steps he took were like months and years of information packed into a few feet, so when he was finally close enough to be within reach, I almost felt like we were already old friends.

There were specks of gold paint in his jet mess of hair. He was painting his apartment, he explained—a karmic move, I'd ultimately learn, as he had broken up with his live-in girlfriend eight months before and was just now getting around to making the place his own again. He told me his cat, Benny, was mesmerized by the change of environment—a shocking gold wall.

Benny was not the only mesmerized cat. We found a corner table to share, and ended up sharing my chocolate, while listening to the music and engaging in the casual game of making each other laugh. When the music stopped and the dishes were cleared, we said goodbye and went our separate ways.

I was intrigued. *Very* intrigued. Intrigued enough to, well, I admit it—to stalk him. It wasn't a conscious plan, but the warm, delicious feeling of being around him drove me to seek out a mutual acquaintance I hadn't spoken with in years. "Where does he live?" I asked this friend. *Damn that new Taurus moon.*

A week later, with the moon in Leo—my sign—and Venus in my house of relationships, I was in an optimistic mood. I climbed up the front stoop of a yellow bungalow apartment in North Hollywood and knocked on the door. If he was surprised to see me, he didn't show it. "Let's get coffee," I chirped. He grabbed his keys and we were off.

Thirteen years later, we're married with children.

Astrologically, it breaks down like this: His Taurus sun sits promptly on my Taurus moon, which is the cosmic equivalent of the famous Hollywood line "You had me at hello." He doesn't have to work very hard to win me, and I'm emotionally vulnerable to the slightest changes in his temperament. I don't have to guess how he's feeling because I feel it, too.

My sun hovers near his natal Venus, so I glow with the nurturing, feminine forces in his universe—the soft, safe places where he opens his heart.

I'm not saying we have the perfect astrological convergence of energies—there is no such thing. What I'm saying is that together, our stars make patterns that keep our relationship exciting and our lives connected.

The stars don't give predictions—people do. It's all in the interpretation. I didn't know that my future husband was going to be in that dinner club that night. I'm glad I didn't know. I prefer to let the mystery of life unfold all on its own. But I do enjoy looking to the stars to provide meaning and context for events after they happen so I can understand the significance of the sweet stuff. You know, like eating soufflés . . . and falling in love.

TAKE CHARGE, LOVERGIRL

So. You want to know what's in all this for you. How do you take control of your own love karma? Okay, I get it. I'll tell you—yes, I'll tell you the secret of how you can make things happen in your own love life. But first let me tell you about my friend Abby.

The suggestion first came from her personal astrologer, yours truly: "Write a love letter," I told her, "from you to you. Try to seduce yourself with it."

Abby, a redheaded hospital administrator from Boston, came to see me about her boyfriend. She and her guy had been together for six months, and although she found him sweet and smart and sexy, she often felt invisible in their relationship. He sometimes appeared interested in other women. He often forgot to call. She suspected that he was getting ready to dump her.

She longed to be longed for, she confided. Longed for, respected, wanted, admired. "Is that too much to ask for?" she demanded.

My answer: *nope*. And to prove it, I gave her this letter-writing remedy. I knew that if she could express appreciation for herself on paper, she would attract the adoring someone of her dreams.

Now, one would think that a romantic pursuit between you and you wouldn't be too hard. How far can you possibly run from yourself? Pretty far, it turns out. In my experience, many clients would rather fall in love with almost anyone over themselves, including criminals, jerks, and losers. Being an ego-lovin' Leo, I can't wrap my head around why the idea of self-infatuation is such a scandal, but I've witnessed a lot of resistance to the notion nonetheless.

That's where the full moon comes in. To help my clients get past what-ever mind-sets have kept them from taking care of number one, I often encourage them to get grooving with the full moon. Because when the full moon is out, we women tend to get a little unleashed, and sometimes, well, that's exactly what we need.

Why does the full moon do this to us? Put it this way: The full moon is a wild woman, a winged Lilith—not to be trusted in polite company! A little racy and a lot selfish, she teases out inhibitions, only to dash them. She isn't satisfied until hearts howl open, primal instincts leap into motion, and danger gets the finger flip. That's why she sets the perfect scene for something as scary as launching a seduction of self.

I said to Abby, "During the upcoming full moon, write yourself a love letter. Don't hold back. Don't feel dumb. And don't be modest. Worship yourself with words, the way you would with someone you're really excited about."

Luckily, Abby is a Sagittarius and tends to be open to outrageous suggestions. So instead of rolling her eyes and running to buy the latest relationship self-help book and a pint of self-pity ice cream, she got busy and wrote herself a kick-ass love letter. And then another. And then a few more. Before she knew it, she was head-over-heels, in-deep, got-it-bad in love with hers truly.

She was also brave enough to share one of her early letters with me. It started out a little stiff and awkward:

You have beautiful hair. That shampoo you use smells good. I appreciate how clean your skin is.

Um, okay. Not exactly rock-my-world letter-writing, but it was a start. And then this fiery Sag caught the spirit of the exercise, and her letter spun into a personal and magical profession of adoration:

I love that you can't keep a secret. It's adorable how much you like to laugh. And you don't give up, do you? Especially if your goal has to do with helping friends. Just when I think you're as wonderful as you can be, you do something to make me realize that you're absolutely determined, unstoppable, and a ton of fun, too.

When I asked Abby how it felt to write that first letter, she said it felt as though someone else had taken over her pen. As though a secret part of her personality was awakened, and it was burning to communicate with the rest of her—to tell her just how loved and cherished she was, and deserved to be.

What's more, it made her realize she didn't want that part of her to be secret anymore. After all, if she didn't even know her own intoxicatingly lovable side, how could her boyfriend be expected to?

It wasn't long before crushing on herself became a habit—and not just when there was a full moon. She put Post-it notes up when the moon was void, too, saying things like, "Rock that big meeting, girl!" and "I am a GENIUS." She traced her own name in notebooks when the moon was hanging out in Sagittarius. She wrote a poem to her number one love— herself—when the skies were totally dark but she wanted to feel lighthearted. She romanced herself, and found that she was a freakin' good catch.

Abby looked to her astrological identity—a Sagittarius sun with a Capricorn moon—to gather clues about how to best appreciate herself. As a Sagittarius, her fiery spirit and willingness to dive into new ideas are coupled with Capricorn moon's emotional discipline, maturity, and ambition. It's a combo of conservative outrageousness, tasteful offense, measured madness. Abby knew she was a powerful woman who, at the same time, didn't need to overshadow her friends' feelings. She could set her aspirations aside when a gal pal needed coffee and sympathy. And she knew she could rise above the trap of being defined by her romantic relationships.

As a newspaper astrology columnist, I get letters from readers mostly on the topic of love. *Will I ever fall in love?* they ask. *Are we compatible, is it true love, will he commit?* And, of course: *When is it going to happen for me?*

To which I reply: Love isn't something that just happens. Or rather, it does just happen, but in the same way that your TiVo just happens to record your favorite show. This command over media is a delight that, after a busy day of work, seems like a random occurrence of natural beauty. However, it can only occur after you've programmed your fab robot and paid the bill.

Programming yourself for love and paying the techno-piper of romance is between you and you. And no matter what your stars suggest, the skies can't make anything happen for you (even if your Venus is in conjunction with your sun in Libra, suggesting that your romantic partners are always within the radius of your remote control). A certain amount of personal responsibility is necessary—the stars are on your side, but *you've* gotta get the job done. And I find that when a woman moves toward creating romance in her life, the stars meet her more than halfway.

Astrology is on your side if you use it well. If you want to add some *ooh-ah oomph* to your personal life, knowing your astrological makeup can give you an edge—by highlighting the secret strengths you possess but may not have explored fully yet. If you don't know what's rockin' about you, consider this your chance to plug your stars into a Marshall amplifier and let them wail your glory song.

That's what Abby did, and it worked for her. But her story doesn't end with a few letters and a newly appreciated sense of self. . . .

One night, a few months after we met, her boyfriend stayed at her apartment. She woke before he did and went out to get groceries for breakfast while he slept. When she came back an hour later, he was sitting on the couch, holding a letter, with tears in his eyes. He wanted to know *who?* And *how long has this been going on?*

She never revealed the actual source of the passionate letter he found, or the source of her blossoming confidence, for that matter.

"It doesn't matter," she said simply, and took him back to bed, where she showed him not only how much she loved him, but also how much she was worthy of his undivided love and affection.

In three months, she had transformed her self-image from feeling invisible to knowing with confidence that she was an ever-present, gorgeous, essential fixture in her man's mind and heart. And the best part was, she didn't have to give up her affair with herself.

It's still going on, I hear.

SOUL MATE STRATEGY

The other question I get asked most often is: *How can I find my soul mate, my intended, my one true love?* Really? I ask back. You haven't found him or her yet? And you're wondering why?

Sure, I'll tell you. Lean in real close and I'll explain it to you. Ready?

He or she does not exist.

Now you hate me. *Thanks a lot, Holiday,* you're thinking. *Crush my dreams, why dontcha?*

Actually, I'm doing you a huge favor. Because if you're out there looking for your one and only soul mate, the sage on your hill, the froth on your frappuccino, you're pretty much guaranteed disappointment. Looking for "the one" puts the death kiss on relationships. It's too much pressure, and it causes us to impose our secret and needy agenda on every prospect we come into contact with, constantly sizing up each candidate with a checklist: "Are you the one? Do you yin my yang? Do you complete me?"

Which is so not sexy.

Trying to control love, or look for it, is the best way to repel it. Venus, which is the love energy, is just like that. It's playful, mischievous, and light, and the minute you apply your rules and list of expectations to it, it goes looking for someone who's more fun.

I hear a lot of desperation and worry from people looking for their mates. And if there is any kind of energy that is the opposite of attraction, that's it. I think it would be a great service to the planetary mood if everyone who is worried about finding their soul mate would just call off the search. The searching energy is actually totally opposite from the energy of attraction that Venus is all about. This gorgeous IT-girl of a planet, who has been admired and worshiped through the ages, is the brightest thing in the sky, save the moon—go out and look. She's all about "come to me, love me, I'm shining here, you can't miss me—and if you do (idiot), you're not the sort for me." So when you're ready to let your inner Venus come out and do her thing, you've got to leave the desperate energy of "searching" and adopt Venus's bright and sassy attitude. Then leave her alone for a while and *just let it happen.*

★ ARIES ★

ARIES ALLURE: When you're "on," everyone around you can feel the force of your personality, which is ruled by Mars. The vitality running through your veins is a magnet for passionate people. But when you're not "on" sparking up your mojo is as difficult as starting a fire with a rock and a stick. Unless you have the inside scoop. . .

HOW TO TURN UP YOUR AQ (ATTRACTION QUOTIENT):

- **Take part in competitions.** The prospect of winning brings out your best qualities and puts them on display for new admirers.
- **Get physical.** An Aries without an exercise routine is missing out on one

of the prime Aries talents—energy to burn. The more you sweat, the more attractive you are post-shower.

- **Travel with a conversation-starter.** You're often brave enough to approach someone you don't know, which is lucky to the extreme.
- **Be open to following.** You're a cardinal sign who wants to initiate. But it's lonely to always be the initiator and never feel what it's like to dance to another person's lead. Your AQ goes up every time you relax and let someone else take control.

WHAT NOT TO DO: Don't come on too strong. You have an influential personality anyway, which requires no magnification. You'd be surprised how much mileage you can get from a subtle innuendo, a raised eyebrow, a well-timed pause. Insinuate instead of speaking frankly. Get in touch with your inner coy. Go diminuendo instead of fortissimo. Think of yourself as a movie actress in a romantic comedy, as opposed to a stage actress in *Long Day's Journey into Night*.

HOW TO SEDUCE AN ARIES MAN: Let him talk about himself endlessly, and then say one fabulously supportive thing before walking away. He'll follow you like he's a puppy and you're holding his food dish.

HOW TO SEDUCE AN ARIES WOMAN: Be the alpha, but do it from afar. Display your strength in an indirect gesture—like carrying some heavy thing from her car, or opening a canned good with your teeth. (Just kidding about the canned good. But try it anyway. She'll probably dig it.) Know that she notices and will think about you. Let her. Do not chase her. Wait for a signal before you make a second move.

YOUR LOVE MANTRA: *People dig me. I don't have to do anything more than be open to love, and it comes to me.*

YOU'RE A SUCKER FOR: flatterers. Sugared words melt your heart. So just make sure the person dealing your ear candy is also strong enough to tell you things you're not as eager to hear—like: "I spent the money in our account on a Stratocaster," "I was really at the Viper Room on Thursday night," or "I'd rather stick needles in my eye than watch one more reality-show rerun with you."

YOUR BEST PICKUP LINE: has no words at all. It's a casual and pleasant once-over that lingers for a millisecond too long to be mistaken for indifference. Followed by an air of indifference.

Rx FOR A BROKEN HEART: Do not say that you'll remain friends with your ex. Jump right back into the dating pool, even if it means spending time with people you'd rather drown than go to a movie with. For you, being annoyed with your choices is part of the healing process.

★ TAURUS ★

TAURUS ALLURE: Sure, you're lusty, salt-of-the-earthy, naturally groovy, and Venus-ruled beauteous. But you're also modest, so you tend to not think of yourself as an object of desire until someone lets you know in no uncertain terms that they want you. But why wait for an admirer when you already have all you need to get in touch with your inner va-va-voom?

HOW TO TURN UP YOUR AQ:

- **Stop pretending you don't know you're magnificent.** It's not a sin to appreciate your fine qualities. Look in the mirror in the morning and give up some praise. Start with a minute's worth and work up to ten. It will feel corny at first, but when you ponder your own exquisite eyeballs and let yourself know that you're a vital, sexy, way-smart babe, it's like turning on an attraction magnet.

- **Realize that Venus blessed you.** You have been sanctified with the sensual awareness and single focus needed to seduce almost anyone you choose to target. However, this is best accomplished indirectly. Oddly, you attract the object of your desire by diverting all of your attention to something other than him or her.

- **Throw yourself entirely into a project.** And make it one that involves using your talent. When you're giving all you've got to "your thing," you are mesmerizing.

WHAT NOT TO DO: Don't stay on one note. Due to your inherent stubbornness, you sometimes realize what works and then press that button until the cows (or bulls, as the case may be) come home. But what's working will cease working if it's overdone. Skillful seductions require artful changes. So maybe one week you're the supportive cheerleader, calling daily to rally him, and that seems to be winning his heart. The next week, play the mysterious sex goddess instead—Greta Garbo him. Follow this act by planning a spa day for two, sharing your knowledge of luxury living. And then what's next? Maybe nothing at all. Maybe something thrilling. Only you know. Keep 'em suspended in wonder.

HOW TO SEDUCE A TAURUS MAN: Be the temptress. Just as one starts to get hungry because one smells the bread baking, you can stimulate the appetite of your intended by providing a glimpse of the pleasures to come.

HOW TO SEDUCE A TAURUS WOMAN: Show her in a subtle way that you appreciate fine qualities and fine things—that you know how to take care of yourself and how to present yourself, and that you understand what it means to be rich in spirit. And smell good. Once she starts with the flirty eyes, you've got her—the rest is cake.

YOUR LOVE MANTRA: *I'm a catch. I'm such a catch that even I am in love with me. I fall only for worthy partners. My love is a rare and luxurious gift.*

YOU'RE A SUCKER FOR: money. And you can spot a millionaire at fifty paces plus—not to mention your uncanny ability to sort the profiles of princes from paupers on Yahoo! Personals. You love being spoiled, but when the bill comes around, you are suddenly practical enough to recognize the overwhelming appeal of OPM (that's other people's money). Don't mistake a wealthy lover for a rich one. True riches cannot be bought. (That said, what's the harm in accepting a nice gift? You don't have to marry someone to appreciate that he sends his personal shopper to Tiffany's for you.)

YOUR BEST PICKUP LINE: "Want chocolate?" Your voracious appetite dictates the contents of your purse, and there's almost always something good in there to share.

Rx FOR A BROKEN HEART: Don't share your chocolate with anyone. Eat it yourself. Let yourself wallow selfishly and slovenly for weeks and weeks, consuming mounds of molten calories while rereading back issues of *Us Weekly*. Then, one hope-filled day, decide to see the light at the end of the gluttonous tunnel. Pick yourself up and head to the gym.

★ GEMINI ★

GEMINI ALLURE: You like it hot. Just like your iconic sex-kitten signmate, Marilyn Monroe—but not in the way everyone thinks. You know what's hip, fun, and now—and that's sexy. Marilyn was a serious intellectual, and it was the brains behind her bubbly personality that made her an unpredictable presence and an unforgettable talent.

HOW TO TURN UP YOUR AQ:

- **Crack jokes.** Or whisper them. Mercury-ruled, your banter is like buttah. You get away with using pointed words by delivering them tenderly. Your sense of humor and mischief is the cornerstone of your appeal—more important than any physical attribute.

- **Keep your intellect tuned up.** Read as much as possible and become a fan of other intellectuals.

- **Blur the lines between friendship and love.** Some of the best relationships in your life will be friendships, then passion, then friendships, then passion. . . . It's like the regular rules don't apply to you. And you're one of those rare people who can maintain a good relationship with an ex.

- **Introduce important people to your posse.** Because your friends are nuts about you, you look your fabulous best in the mirror of their admiration.

★ Astrological Question ★

"I'm madly in love with a Capricorn girl born on Christmas. Her ex left her, and she is having a hard time getting over him. We dated for six months, and she now wants time off to get over her feelings for the other man. I'm a Gemini. Do you see us getting back together?"

Sorry, Gemini. She's a Capricorn woman, and she has already made up her mind. Lyle Lovett even wrote a song called "She's Already Made Up Her Mind" that explains it all: "There is nothing so unwavering as a Capricorn woman / When she's already made up her mind." Okay, I may have added the Capricorn part. But don't give up just yet. There is hope. Use your Gemini charm—on another woman. Yes! Capricorn gals are fiercely competitive, and she'll probably fight to get you back. (Don't lead this other woman on, though. That's not only bad karma, it's just plain old bad manners.)

WHAT NOT TO DO: Don't stay in when you could be out. Circulating in the world helps you maintain your edge. Besides, one of the reasons you are so interesting is that you're so interested. (Some bullies call you fickle. But isn't being fickle really just a form of open-mindedness?) When you let one of your many interests carry you to classes, museums, new restaurants, different countries, and fresh social circles, you can't help but attract admirers along the way.

HOW TO SEDUCE A GEMINI MAN: Play your opposites. Employ both sides of your twinny personality to create a fascinating dichotomy. Be simultaneously sassy and soft. Play the bad nun, the angelic bitch, the sophisticated farm girl, or the compassionate dominatrix. Have fun with your various roles!

HOW TO SEDUCE A GEMINI WOMAN: Verbally spar with her—it's how she determines your worthiness. However, if you disagree with her, do it in a way that doesn't insult her. Note: The best way to disagree is to really agree, but to voice your agreement in a way that sounds like you're disagreeing.

YOUR LOVE MANTRA: *I'm a sharp-tongued goddess. A wisecracking wonder woman. A fabulous female. Anyone who doesn't get me just isn't smart enough.*

YOU'RE A SUCKER FOR: fresh meat. The new person on the scene has the power to titillate and enrapture you—for at least a week and a half. Then, if this person doesn't step up the game or overwhelm you in some amazing way, you're on to the next affair du jour.

YOUR BEST PICKUP LINE: "It's time we met." Your breezy style gets him guessing whether you're flirting or just being friendly. The uncertainty keeps him hooked.

Rx FOR A BROKEN HEART: Get smarter. Not about love—about anything else. Learn about clouds or famous women in history, learn about fashion design or calculus. The "what" doesn't matter—you can find something fascinating about any subject—it's just the fact that you're engaged in something other than your heartache. While your brain is fed, your heart will have a chance to heal.

★ CANCER ★

CANCER ALLURE: You're a mother. Even if you're not a mother and never plan to be, you're a mother. Your nurturing spirit attracts those who need healing and compassion—and who doesn't in some way or another? And though you don't always deliver your remedies in a sweet or sensitive way, your toughness only adds to your magnetism. You genuinely care. And that's why they surrender their hearts to you.

HOW TO TURN UP YOUR AQ:

- **Commune with others who have similar spiritual beliefs.** Whether it's at church, at school, or in nature, sharing your spiritual journey (even if that comes in the form of debating instead of celebrating) brings you new friends and love.
- **Get your instrumental groove on.** Making music by plucking, strumming, bowing, or blowing adds considerable attraction points. Even more so if you become good enough to showcase your talent at gatherings or on a stage.
- **Bring 'em back to your place.** It's where you shine. Your beautifully arranged abode is even more of a refuge for you when you let it be a place of comfort for worthy friends and loved ones.

WHAT NOT TO DO: Don't get wiggy. Your tendency to change your feelings with the shifting moon can be delightfully unpredictable or just plain scary. Acting on every feeling that flickers across your heart is unwise. (By the way, so is driving by his house repeatedly, texting under the influence, or emailing after midnight.) Be judicious.

HOW TO SEDUCE A CANCER MAN: Cook for him. Your sweets are divine, your savories, salivational! Besides, you look simply marvelous in an apron.

HOW TO SEDUCE A CANCER WOMAN: Be the rock. Highlight all the ways you are emotionally even and solid. She desires someone who isn't afraid of an occasional emotional outburst from someone—who is calm even in the midst of chaos. And here's a fun trick that will win her: Create a little piece of harmless chaos, and then be very calm in the midst of it.

YOUR LOVE MANTRA: *I don't have to be tough all the time. My vulnerability makes me poetic, romantic, and enchanting. It's safe to be me, as is.*

YOU'RE A SUCKER FOR: a full-grown problem child. If he misbehaves, comes across as terribly broken, or is just plain immature, you can't resist thinking that he's on the brink of a change and just needs a good woman to show him the way. And it may actually be true—if anyone can do it, you can. However, what a lot of work. Yeesh!

YOUR BEST PICKUP LINE: "My place or mine?" Okay, maybe it's not the first thing you should say, but it is wonderful to be admired in your element, even if it's in a casual, friendly way. If the book club is meeting at your house, or you're having a garage sale or game night, invite your romantic prospect to join you.

Rx FOR A BROKEN HEART: Stay home. For as many hours in the day as you possibly can without getting fired. Stay on the couch until the remote has adhered itself to your palm and dust bunnies have formed under you. Pity yourself until it annoys your friends, freaks out your family, and incites even your therapist to threaten to dump you. Cry until your sinuses swell and your eyes puff shut. In approximately twenty-eight days (a complete lunar cycle), you'll feel almost totally better.

LEO ALLURE: You are a performer at heart. You are never so glorious as when you're in the spotlight, so honing your appeal is a matter of getting your show on the road. Whether it's telling a good joke, singing, making a toast, or taking over the dance floor, be ready to launch into your "act" at the slightest provocation.

HOW TO TURN UP YOUR AQ:

- **Be totally unaware of your powers of attraction.** The thing about people with "It" is that they often don't know they have It. And this enables them to use It and wield It mercilessly.
- **Be overly generous.** Even when you're afraid that to do so would be inappropriate—it could be for others, but you wear even foolish generosity well. So gush away, gift until you can wrap no more, share your boisterous spirit with the whole world.
- **Listen more than you talk.** This is how you learn what people like and dislike. Being in touch with the entertainment appetites of your potential fans helps you delight them time and again.

★ Astrological Question ★

I'm a Leo woman in a relationship with another Leo woman. You would think that two people of the same sex and of the same sign would understand love in the same way, but we don't. She says she loves me, but I'm just not feeling it from her. Should we break up?"

One of my mentors, the urban mystic Stuart Wilde, enlightened me on the nature of love when he said, "Love is a quality of attention. It's a way of focusing on someone." When you are focusing on someone in a loving way, that is love. In that light, someone who is behaving in an unloving way and claiming "But I love you…" is at best confused and at worst manipulative. Leos are beautifully demonstrative people. If your Leo girlfriend is often demonstrating to you something that feels quite opposite from support, friendship, kindness, spiritual generosity and care, then in those instances she does not love you. So educate her. Perhaps things will shift. And if they don't, then I say bail.

WHAT NOT TO DO: Don't hog the spotlight. Yes, shine in your moment. Then, in true vaudevillian style, swing your arms to the side and say, "Take it away, Bob" (or Jim, or Fred, or whoever). And then watch while said person takes his solo.

HOW TO SEDUCE A LEO MAN: Play pretend games. Leo men love a chance to perform, especially as some dormant part of their personality. I'm not suggesting you dress up as the naughty cheerleader and cast him in the role of the head quarterback or anything like that. But if you were to privately cast yourself in the role of the sophisticated intellectual, he might naturally fall into the role of the eager student—or the worldly mentor. And if you were to subliminally assign yourself the role of the princess in distress, he might slay a dragon for you.

HOW TO SEDUCE A LEO WOMAN: Believe in love at first sight and convince yourself, and then her, that it is exactly what is happening between the two of you. Do not hold back or play it cool. Overwhelm her with your adoration. Then, once you're sure she's hooked, hold back and play it cool. Let her feel the unbearable loss of you. And when she reaches for you, pour on the affection again.

YOUR LOVE MANTRA: *I'm a gracious queen. I lavish others with amorous attention, and deserve every bit of queenly attention I receive in return.*

YOU'RE A SUCKER FOR: withholders. If they're moody, broody, and too self-involved to applaud at the end of most of your sentences, you're intrigued enough to follow them around for a while, trying to win them. Perhaps this is because you're so used to people wanting to join your fan club after five minutes of your one-woman show. (And don't say, "What one woman show?" You know what I'm talking about. You're probably doing it right now, you diva, you.)

YOUR BEST PICKUP LINE: "Break a leg!" Because usually the people you are interested in are doing some kind of show of their own.

Rx FOR A BROKEN HEART: Love is both the disease and the remedy. Sure, right now maybe you'd rather flow anthrax than blessings to your offending party. However, you'll be on to having fun, romance, and passion in your life quickly if you can simply wish your ex well.

★ VIRGO ★

VIRGO ALLURE: You are the sign of the Real Deal. You are the Genuine Article, the Original Member. Authenticity is your sexiest quality, and unlike other here-today-gone-tomorrow attributes, authenticity never goes out of style. It may take longer for others to notice what an astounding beauty you are, as you possess an attraction that grows. However, usually it's the crème de la crème who immediately fall for your subtle and lingering charms.

HOW TO TURN UP YOUR AQ:

- **Embrace your inner nerd.** (Who are we fooling? For most of you, your nerd was outed years ago. In that case, embrace your outer nerd.) Well-directed obsession has been sexy ever since Bill Gates dropped out of college to change the world by getting geeky in his parents' garage. Of course, it doesn't matter if you're into writing code, growing orchids, or looking at microbes under a microscope. It's the dedication and mad specificity you apply to your hobbies that wing your AQ into the stratosphere.

- **Hang out with baddies, crazies, or generally irritating people.** It's no secret that you like a routine and a relatively calm, controlled environment. So it's important that you're regularly exposed to people who surprise you and push the boundaries of what you consider to be acceptable. (A class of preschoolers, a table of cigar-smoking poker players, or your family should do just fine.) Disruptive influences not only challenge you to be tolerant, they inspire you and keep you fresh.

- **Priss it up.** Don't worry about coming across as prudish if something doesn't feel right to you. No one will think any less of you if you stick to your values even when the cool kids are smoking in the bathroom—or whatever the grown-up version of that may be. Your integrity makes you more than cool—it makes you hot.

WHAT NOT TO DO: Don't be a backseat driver. Ditch the know-it-all tone, and deny your urge to nag. Most people don't like to be told what to do, especially when they are on a date. And the type of person who does like to be told what to do is probably someone you won't respect. It's okay to let those you love, or are merely interested in, make mistakes on your dime. Who knows? The screw-ups could be more fun than everything going so-called "right."

HOW TO SEDUCE A VIRGO MAN: Impress him with your nurturing spirit. Let him see how kind you are to small children in restaurants. Let him catch you in the act of gardening the bejesus out of those delicate tomato plants. Let him experience your fab chicken soup when he's under the weather.

HOW TO SEDUCE A VIRGO WOMAN: Pay attention. Notice things about her that nobody else does. Remember facts that she told you in passing. Then bring them back into conversation days or weeks later. She longs to be so important to someone that they ruminate over her tiniest offhand gesture. Be that someone.

YOUR LOVE MANTRA: *My romantic karma is so spotless that even my soul gleams. I deserve every pleasurable romantic experience I create.*

YOU'RE A SUCKER FOR: a makeover opportunity. If his visage screams "before," you're hoppin' eager to get him to "after." And perhaps you can change the world to a more date-friendly place, one head-to-toe revamp at a time. Just be careful to choose subjects that either want to be made over or at least have the decency to feel improved.

YOUR BEST PICKUP LINE (to be said with a Mae West–ian shrug of the shoulder): "Come on up and see me—and my extensive and impressive array of cleaning products—sometime."

Rx FOR A BROKEN HEART: Sparkle your world. Scrub like a hotel maid on speed. Donate like the Red Cross. Destroy like an arsonist. Shred paper, move furniture, empty drawers, buy new sheets, paint. When the last wineglass is shining and there's not a speck of dust left on the floorboards, you'll finally feel normal again.

★ LIBRA ★

LIBRA ALLURE: You are the Venus-proclaimed purveyor of good taste. Which extends, naturally, to your love life. You can take something as messy as love and turn it into something that smells good, looks fantastic, and works like a dream—so long as it's the right person. As the sign of partnership, you're always looking for the perfect fit and have no problem going for long stints without dating at all, because you're so picky that you'd rather date no one than someone you're not that into.

HOW TO TURN UP YOUR AQ:

- **Make your environment lovely to behold in your own eyes.** This includes the environment of your body, your clothes, your home, your car, and so on. When your physical world is the way you like it, you begin to feel inner peace, and vice versa. In the end it's that sense of peace (and not the physical trappings you've perfected) that potential loves can't resist.

- **Accept what you can't change.** Though your too-good-to-be-true personality will draw people in, it's your humanness that bonds them to you. Knowing that, for all your fabulosity, you're just as screwy as other mortals makes others want to get close to you.

- **Accept what you could, but don't, change.** For whatever reason, if you haven't done it yet, you may not need to at all. If getting your degree, losing weight, or learning how to cook has had more play on your New Year's resolution list than a *Sex and the City* rerun on cable, maybe it's time to stop the quest. Non-improvement will actually be an improvement, because it frees you to stop harping on yourself and start finding endeavors that are so compelling to you, you simply can't help but get going on them. And that's when you're at your sexy best.

WHAT NOT TO DO: Don't waffle. Libra is renowned for taking forever to make a decision. But once it's made, it's usually right for the time. Whether it's as simple as a haircut or as complex as where to live or whom to love, Libra needs only to believe in the validity of a decision so that wonderful things can be born of that choice. Certainty is sexy.

HOW TO SEDUCE A LIBRA MAN: Be impeccably put together. His refined visual sense keeps him turned on by clean lines, simple elegance, and artistic balance. Note: You don't have to have a perfect body or face to pull this off. It's your skillful and thoughtful presentation of what you've got that keeps him breathlessly alert.

HOW TO SEDUCE A LIBRA WOMAN: Fall under her spell. Allow yourself to be absorbed by her opinions and taken in by her taste. Accommodate and praise her choices. Mirror her gestures. Agree. She will let down her guard and let you into her heart.

YOUR LOVE MANTRA: *I can trust myself to make the right decision. And if it's not right, I can always change my mind.*

YOU'RE A SUCKER FOR: aristocracy. You're titillated by well-bred men whose social graces make them impossible to read. Your knees go weak when you discover that their grandmother was a duchess, or that they've been documented in the society pages. And if their hands are soft, indicating that the hardest work they do is lift a telephone, all the better.

YOUR BEST PICKUP LINE: "Do you know how to get to Sixth Street?" Your sense of direction is questionable—just another way your sign's tendency toward indecision plays out. But it's a darn good excuse to roll down your window and engage that hottie in the Prius next to you in a little eye contact.

Rx FOR A BROKEN HEART: Immerse yourself in artistic greatness. Visit museums, read books, associate with artistic people. Chances are, most of the art you respond to was made by someone who has been similarly heartbroken and creates from the depths of that pain. If they can turn their personal tragedy into something beautiful, so can you.

★ SCORPIO ★

SCORPIO ALLURE: your heat. Of all the signs of the zodiac, Scorpio is the most naturally in touch with her inner sizzle—and she may turn that burner up or down, but she rarely turns it off. She gets that being sexy isn't about wearing mascara or being the right shape or saying the right thing; sexy is in the blood. And all one has to do to be sexy is accept that one already *is* sexy.

HOW TO TURN UP YOUR AQ:

- **Get spiritual.** A magical, mystical power emanates from you when you are feeling connected to that which cannot be seen but can be nonetheless

★ SHE'S A SCORPIO ★

Rolling Stone magazine lauded folk icon JONI MITCHELL as one of the greatest songwriters ever. Ever! And no one's arguing. To contain the poetic complexities of human existence in a simple song is a lifetime aspiration of most musicians. So how does Joni Mitchell seem to do it every time? First of all, any Scorpio worth the salt in her seawater is committed to noticing the multiple layers of consciousness that affect every aspect of life. Scorpio is about the currents, the undercurrents, and the under-undercurrents. In other words, Scorpio is deep— so deep that she realizes and celebrates that everything and everyone is deep.

profoundly experienced. Therefore, meditation, prayer, and reflection are as important to your sex appeal as exercise, diet, fashion, and anything else in the physical realm.

- **Keep a love journal.** Make this a secret book in which you talk to your own heart. You will be surprised at the wild poetry that runs through your veins. Putting something in your journal a few times a week, regardless of who is or isn't in your love life, also helps you consciously create the kind of romance you would love to have.

- **Know and wear your signature scent.** Scorpio has a heightened and primal attunement to the role of scent in attraction. You know when someone smells right to you, so it's important to smell right to yourself. Maybe your personal scent is a favorite perfume, but it doesn't have to be—it could be oil, soap, shampoo, pheromones, lotion, the way you naturally smell after playing tennis, or just the fact that you like to carry an orange in your purse.

WHAT NOT TO DO: Don't try to be nice. When you're not genuinely feeling it, you just can't pull off the act. Instead of covering your feelings, lead with them. The salty, opinionated, irreverent you will probably be a bigger hit than Nicey anyway.

HOW TO SEDUCE A SCORPIO MAN: Bring Naughty You to the party. Chances are there's very little you could do that he would find distasteful, so unlock the figurative handcuffs of your imagination. (Paradoxically, you may find this easiest to do while locking actual handcuffs to the bedpost.)

HOW TO SEDUCE A SCORPIO WOMAN: Be the most obviously intriguing and hilarious person in the room, and appear to not care a lick about what other people think. She likes 'em funny, witty, irreverent, and completely unself-conscious. Then make a discreet play for her attention—perhaps a note or a text message. Secret messages turn her on.

YOUR LOVE MANTRA: *Truth is sexy. The more willing I am to see and reflect the truth, the sexier I am.*

YOU'RE A SUCKER FOR: the loner. You assume he isolates himself because he's such good company that he likes to have his own undivided attention. You attribute his brooding to his being deep. You attribute his unkempt hair to his being a nonconformist. You infuse his grunts with meaning. And sometimes you're right—he's the genius catch of the century. And other times he's the Unabomber.

YOUR BEST PICKUP LINE: "I had the weirdest dream last night." Your fascination with the subconscious is a participatory sport and an invitation to others to share their own surreal lives. And you're keen enough to interpret and use the information you garner.

Rx FOR A BROKEN HEART: Write comedy. Yes, as in stand-up! Don't worry, you don't have to sign up for open mic night or anything like that—yet. But forcing yourself to see the annoying, painful, and weird things about your relationship as downright funny, and documenting them as such, not only will lift your spirits but will empower you.

★ SAGITTARIUS ★

SAGITTARIUS ALLURE: your timing. Being able to capture the heart and imagination of a desirable partner is often a matter of timing. And your sexiest quality is just that—a fabulous knack for putting your finger on the "it" moment. This comes across in your humor, in the way you skillfully direct a seduction, and in your tasteful social charms. And with lucky Jupiter as your guiding planet, you often find yourself drawn quite naturally to the right place at the right moment, standing next to the right person and wearing the right outfit.

HOW TO TURN UP YOUR AQ:

- **Take advantage of opportunity!** What use is good luck if you don't follow through? For instance, when you hit it off with new people, be the first to call and establish the relationship beyond the original circumstance that brought you together.
- **Channel your fiery passion into mundane tasks.** You never know whom you'll run into while washing the car or going on a daily jog.

- **Let your inklings lead the way.** The point where curiosity meets intuition usually has the potential to begin a mission. And you are sexiest when on a mission.

WHAT NOT TO DO: Don't be fickle. There's a difference between spontaneity and flakiness. You can honor your commitments and be a free spirit at the same time.

HOW TO SEDUCE A SAGITTARIUS MAN: Play up your differences. Keep in mind that his ideal woman is here on a working visa. But you don't have to be from another country to be from another world. Let him in on the unique pieces of your personal culture—your nutty family traditions, an unusual aspect of your education, an exotic food you love to eat—that are oh so different from his own culture.

HOW TO SEDUCE A SAGITTARIUS WOMAN: Make her travel to be with you—if not in reality, then at least in her mind. Tell her things about yourself that she has to stretch her imagination in order to understand. And take her places that make her believe that the world is more exotic and varied than she ever dreamed. She will be intoxicated by the newness you represent.

YOUR LOVE MANTRA: *It's all about excitement. And I can always find some-thing thrilling about the relationship I'm in, whether it's a relationship I've been in for five minutes or twenty-five years.*

YOU'RE A SUCKER FOR: aliens. Not the green kind with the big heads. I'm talking about the exchange student—or anyone who fits that profile in a post–high school kind of way. He's adaptable, he's unfamiliar, and since he doesn't know you or anyone you know, you can be anyone you want around him. How glamorous!

YOUR BEST PICKUP LINE: "Sprechen sie English?" (or any number of inter-national variations thereof). You're always enchanting when you're out of your element, and you're equally charmed by anyone openhearted enough to speak to a perfect stranger like you.

Rx FOR A BROKEN HEART: Travel—like, duh. What did you think I was going to say? Travel is your answer for everything. Lose the family pet? Book a trip to Tibet. Divorce? Tahiti, of course. Best friend run off with your man? How about Japan? There's just something about having a boarding pass in your pocket that turns the world into your Sugaki oyster with a side of ponzu sauce.

★ℭAPRICORN★

CAPRICORN ALLURE: power over others. Allure is about affecting others so profoundly that they are inexplicably pulled in by the connection between you. And Capricorns can do this in their sleep. You were born to lead, and what is a leader if not a person who can create a desire in others and mobilize them to a common end? Sometimes that common end is simply to recognize and respect your irresistible appeal.

HOW TO TURN UP YOUR AQ:

- **Be merciful with your romantic power.** Power, if abused, is fleeting. Romantic power, if abused, usually flees arm in arm with someone wearing a miniskirt.
- **Make fun a priority.** Your workaholic tendencies may make you rich, but it's your funaholic tendencies that will make you a good date. Have at least five activities that you love to do that are in no way related to how you earn money. And do at least one of them every week.
- **Put your style stamp on everything you do.** You tend to be results oriented. But *how* you get things done is really more important than *what* you get done. Approaching even mundane tasks with great and fanciful gusto makes you feel like a winner. And you can use the previous sentence as an explanation when anyone asks why you're sharpening your pencil while wearing a tiara.

WHAT NOT TO DO: Don't compete with your partner or potential partner. A little friendly competition may create the kind of romantic tension that works well in sitcoms, but in real life the laugh track won't kick in after the punch line and your guy will just wind up feeling feeble in the presence of your aggression.

HOW TO SEDUCE A CAPRICORN MAN: Be a Bond Girl—independent and dangerous, and with an agenda. Since Capricorn men like to think of themselves as the shaken-not-stirred type, they like a refined woman they can't quite figure out.

HOW TO SEDUCE A CAPRICORN WOMAN: Own a company that has mutual interests with the company that she owns. In the rare case where neither you nor she owns a company, then talk about the companies that you will own someday, and about what a new and improved, exciting world it will be when the two of you rule it.

YOUR LOVE MANTRA: *I'm willing to surrender to the ride of romance. I'm powerful enough to cede control once in a while to the people I trust.*

YOU'RE A SUCKER FOR: the boss. And he doesn't have to be *your* boss, either. He just has to be in charge of people, and pretty good at it. And if he also dresses pretty well for the position, he gets extra points. Because you're also a sucker for a zesty necktie.

YOUR BEST PICKUP LINE: "Can I count on your vote?" You're always involved in some kind of cause, be it a work project in need of publicity, a community issue that could use support, or your own presidential campaign.

Rx FOR A BROKEN HEART: No, it's not revenge. Of all the signs, you are the most prone to *wanting* revenge. And yet everyone knows that it's impossible to move on with your life and still be spending hours every day posting maniacal comments on Don'tDateHimGirl.com. So when vengeful thoughts start to fill your head, try to remember that the best revenge is always being fabulously over the whole thing. (While the second-best revenge is always dating his closest friend.)

★AQUARIUS★

AQUARIUS ALLURE: unique beauty. Who needs cosmetics when you've got your own cosmic beauty recipe? It's one part zany, one part eccentric, three parts scary-smart. I still can't figure out if Aquarius is living in her own world or is transforming the world wherever she goes. Either way, it's clear that the Aquarian reality is vastly different from the one other people know—and that is what is so deliciously attractive about this sign.

HOW TO TURN UP YOUR AQ:

• **Get social.** As the official social director of the zodiac, your megawatt attraction magnet comes from creating social scenarios in which you can shine. Whether it's to a dreamy date, a fabulous party, or an outrageous event, the friends you invite become enamored with you.

- **Limit your exposure to negativity.** Even if it means you have to forgo the news. When you're up, everyone is up. So stay up as often and for as long as possible. It's kind of like a responsibility that you bear. You don't necessarily have to be a cheerleader, but when things get dim and there's not a happy thought in the room, it's on you to think one. Your eternal optimism is sexy.

- **Schedule regular alone time.** You must replenish your mojo. Long solo walks, shopping sprees, and meditation are some of the things that keep you in the giving spirit your sign is so famous for. And everyone loves a giver.

WHAT NOT TO DO: Don't believe what you hear about other people. The reason you are able to make and keep so many friends is that you stay out of gossip circles and make up your own mind about people. Basing your opinions on your personal experience instead of on hearsay makes you a rare and cherished friend.

HOW TO SEDUCE AN AQUARIUS MAN: Have a better gadget than he does, and use it like a seasoned hacker. He cannot resist a chick who can text without looking at the phone keys. He salivates over a gal who has outfitted her laptop with voice recognition. And he's whipped on the babe who keeps videos of her friends on her iPod.

HOW TO SEDUCE AN AQUARIUS WOMAN: Be unique and unlike anyone she has ever met, but do this with an air of familiarity. Entice her with your knowledge, your worldview, and your vision of the future. And be fascinated by her knowledge, worldview, and vision of the future. Then, when she's least expecting it, call her "a genius."

YOUR LOVE MANTRA: *I let my desire drive my romantic destiny. I can take it from friendship to love whenever I want to. It's safe to bond deeply with others.*

YOU'RE A SUCKER FOR: the power-couple fantasy. If he brings all kinds of side perks, such as a swanky job, a groovy set of friends, and clout in certain impressive arenas, you enjoy dreaming of what a smash hit you'll make on the scene by combining your resources. Unfortunately, there's no tangible evidence that this has anything to do with real love, unless, of course, you count tabloid references to Hollywood couples so hot their names have been blended together as tangible evidence.

YOUR BEST PICKUP LINE: "Hey, you wanna sit with us?" Since you usually roll with your posse, there's a good chance he'll meet you in your own crowd. By talking to him, you make him feel accepted by the whole gaggle.

Rx FOR A BROKEN HEART: Party. As often as possible. Go to lots of them. It really doesn't matter what kind—rooftop party, kid's birthday party,

Tupperware party, party to a crime, party like it's 1999 . . . what matters most is that you're where people are celebrating. And even when you're in a brokenhearted state, you're still susceptible to being caught up in the spirit.

★ PISCES ★

PISCES ALLURE: Should spiritual alignment really be glamorous? Why, of course! Clear pores have nothing on clear karma. And who needs gleaming teeth when you can harness the Great Light to shine through your inner being? Short of putting fake eyelashes on your third eye, you find ways to incorporate a spiritual bent into even the most fanciful vanities. After all, god, or goddess, as the case may be, is beauty. When you calm yourself and connect to your great source, you build up a kind of force field around you, which you can use to attract just the people who interest you.

HOW TO TURN UP YOUR AQ:

- **Accept yourself as a work-in-progress.** It's through your humanity, not through your perfection, that you bond with others. When you can let go of needing to do things right, you're sexier. People feel they can be themselves around you. When you're relaxed and others are relaxed, the magic sets in.

★ ASTROLOGICAL QUESTION ★

"Never one to go from relationship to relationship, I have not been seriously involved with anyone since my marriage broke up five years ago. Now I think I'm ready for a serious commitment to someone special, but I'm not sure. Do you think I'm ready? I'm a Pisces."

I don't think you're ready for a so-called "serious relationship," but I would advise a humorous relationship, a whimsical relationship, a relationship that could never work out in a million years, followed by a relationship that lasts approximately three weeks.

In other words, lighten up! As a Pisces, you can relate to people from all walks of life, at least for a limited period of time, and what you'll learn about yourself in the process will give you the confidence to trust your choices when it's really important. So date wide instead of deep. Think of dating as a chance to, while making new friends and sharing interesting environments and experiences, develop your relationship with your lifelong mate—YOU!

- **Take pleasure and delight in caring for yourself.** Being interested in the latest trends in self-care doesn't mean that you're shallow. Your exterior should reflect your interior. The work and money that go into beauty don't distract one iota from your spiritual practice.
- **Choose your company carefully.** Very, very, *very* carefully. You're the most impressionable sign of the zodiac—which is one of the reasons why you learn so quickly, and often learn the hard way. If other people in your life are telling you that someone is bad for you, listen. They may be right.

WHAT NOT TO DO: Don't impose your beliefs on others. What works for you won't work for everyone. Trust that people may know what's right for them. Besides, there's nothing alluring about superiority.

HOW TO SEDUCE A PISCES MAN: Make a play for him on the astral plane. If you have never consciously traveled to the astral plane, don't worry—it's easier to get there than you think. And it's a super-fun place for seduction (no birth control necessary). All you have to do is get quiet, breathe deeply, and project yourself into an alterna-reality. Then meet him and converse, or whatever, and come back. The next time you see him in this reality, he'll feel inexplicably closer to you.

HOW TO SEDUCE A PISCES WOMAN: Meet her in a yoga class, in a new-age bookstore, or at a lecture on unity consciousness. Be enchanted with her lithe spirit, her bright aura, and her philosophical savvy. Tell her you have a girlfriend (she wants what she can't have) while you continue to build a deep friendship with her. Continue to be charmingly platonic until you are sure she has fallen madly in love with you. Then . . . it's all you, baby.

YOUR LOVE MANTRA: *I can be utterly in love* and *utterly independent. What is for my own best and highest good is also for the best and highest good of those I love.*

YOU'RE A SUCKER FOR: a guru. If a person seems to have a line on some kind of spiritual calling that's out of your earshot, you assume this person is onto something and think you should follow. Perhaps. But ask a skeptical Virgo for an outside opinion, just to be sure. In California, where I live, people often mistake super-hot guys for enlightened beings. Don't make this mistake with your love life.

YOUR BEST PICKUP LINE: "This is my favorite song! What's yours?" This isn't just a line to use at concerts. It also works in reference to the music coming over the grocery store intercom, the tune blasting from your car stereo, or even the whisper of the wind atop a lonely hill. (Note: If you are atop a lonely hill and you happen upon a man you've not met previously, deliver this line while keeping one hand on your pepper spray.)

Rx FOR A BROKEN HEART: Go to the movies. Happy movies, sad movies, critically acclaimed movies, bad movies. While you lose yourself in the characters (which is something you do better than anyone), you gain perspective on your own problems. Little by little your situation, your burdens, and your heart get lighter.

★ hot and heavenly

SEX AND INTIMACY

I met my friend Zoey for coffee one morning a few weeks ago. Though we both ordered nonfat lattes, Zoey didn't need the caffeine, because she was pre-buzzed about her new boyfriend. I'm a good friend, so I listened . . . and listened . . . and listened some more . . . about how smart he is, fab job, fun friends, chin like chiseled marble, mind of a "super-kind shark," Ya-dee-diddle-diddley-yada.

★ She was obviously in deep, and I was happy for her, listening patiently to every detail the way a good friend must when her girlfriend is flung over the moon by a strapping member of the male species.

Then she said, "And tonight's the night. I know it. And I am going to be *reh-dee*." After our coffee date, she said, she was heading straight to the spa, where she planned to get patted, powdered, painted, plucked, perfumed, preened, and prettified. She had also picked out a musical playlist for the evening (heavy on the Led Zeppelin with some Usher thrown in to keep it fresh) and the culinary aphrodisiac (oysters and molten chocolate lava cake). She had even bought new silky sheets for her four-poster bed.

"I'm ready for anything," she said with a wink, "if you know what I mean." Yeah, I knew what she meant. Part of me was tempted to shriek, "TMI! TMI!" right there in the café, but the good friend in me resisted, and I listened patiently as she imparted the details of her plan for her own personal Night to Remember. And, of course, the next day I called her for a postcoital review. (Don't all good friends do that?)

Except . . . nothing happened.

They barely kissed goodnight. She lost the moment. Or maybe he froze. Ian was a Gemini, so it was hard to tell if he was really chicken or if he actually had a million things to do in the morning, which he listed with chatty conviction. Zoey told me that she dropped lots of hints over dinner, but he didn't seem to pick up on them. So when they got back to her place and she lit some candles and put Usher's "Nice and Slow" on the stereo, before she knew it, Mr. Air Sign had flown the coop in a flurry of excuses.

"No worries," I told her. "Gemini guys are easily spooked by preparation and ritual leading up to sex. They think it means something is expected of them, and they're not sure what it is or if they can deliver it. Actually, his leaving so quickly is a sign that he really digs you and doesn't want to disappoint you."

"So what do I do?" she asked, sounding like she was actually taking notes.

"Recognize his need for casual spontaneity. Though you, as a Capricorn chick, find comfort in rituals like head-to-toe beauty procedures, special clothes, sheets, music, and lighting, he's different. His ideal first romp with you probably has an unexpected feel to it, like you just happened to be working out together, going for a run, say, and suddenly you're back at his place, getting all dirty in the shower. Like it just happened and he didn't have to think about it. Geminis are Mercury ruled and are easily muddled up by too much mental info—a buzzkill when it comes to getting down to biz."

"But what about what I need?" Zoey protested.

"For now," I told her, "do your own private sex rituals, but don't involve him. Don't let him see the work—be like a magician creating an illusion of spontaneity. Then let him have it his spur-of-the-moment, casual way—at least until he gets over the first-time jitters. After it all goes well on his terms, he'll be able to relax at your place and appreciate the sexy ambience you've created," I assured her.

When she hung up, she sounded skeptical, but promised to give it a try.

So. Did my advice work? Well, put it this way: It took me a few weeks to get in touch with Zoey again, as she was in what she later described blissfully as an "early honeymoon situation." When she finally did resurface, she didn't have much to say about her recent activities—a nice Capricorn doesn't kiss and tell—but, judging from her look of glowing exhaustion, she was ecstatically oversexed.

# ★ ARIES ★

GODDESS BEHIND CLOSED DOORS: You're no shrinking violet. In fact, you've been known to bare things as a way of bringing a guy closer—your intentions, your ta-tas, but not your soul. Not until he proves himself to be worthy of being taken into your confidence.

You're physically strong, which makes it fun for you to try athletic moves in the bedroom—helicopter, anyone? And you don't even mind if they don't exactly work out, because for you it's all about getting good and sweaty and trying new things.

You can be aggressive and overpowering sometimes. This you do with your attitude—no dominatrix gear necessary. Your ferocity can be fun with the right partner at the right time. But be judicious. Keep it in check. After all, you're not out to scare anyone. Then again, if he's behaving in a chickenlike manner, perhaps he's just not strong enough (cue your get-it-on song). . . .

- **Aries get-it-on song:** "Strong Enough," by Sheryl Crow.
- **Aries favorite time for amore:** first thing in the morning.
- **Aries aphrodisiac:** a duel. But if you happen to not be living in the 18th century, then something like a duel—for instance, two grown men behaving like children as they fight over you.

INTIMACY AND THE ARIES MAN: He's a fighter, not a lover. Don't hold it against him—it's in his DNA to be a conqueror, and you wouldn't want him any other way. He's sexiest when he embraces his warrior spirit and doesn't try to hide it behind a Mr. Nicey mask. That means being bold and sometimes shockingly direct. He respects a gal who can hold her own in games of love and who makes the chase challenging. But when the decathlon of romance is played out, the real gold medalist is a woman who is so confident in her femininity that she doesn't have to compete. And he might not admit it, but her strength turns him all melty on the inside—okay, so maybe he's a fighter and a lover.

★ TAURUS ★

GODDESS BEHIND CLOSED DOORS: With Venus as your planetary parent, sensuality is your first language. You were born to experience pleasure and you know what you want. Furthermore, you have a voracious appetite. You don't want a little of what you want; you want it all. Your love life is therefore usually a feast-or-famine situation.

You find it particularly pleasing to mix your passions up into one big love feast. For instance, chocolate seems like a natural thing to want to eat off another person's body, and doing it in a whirlpool, or on a bed of flower petals—or in a whirlpool of flower petals, for that matter—doesn't seem the least bit elaborate.

You're also picky and easily turned off. It can be anything, really—a thought you can't let go of, a comment made earlier in the evening that replays, a bad smell, a quick move you disapprove of—and once you get turned off, it's super challenging to get back into a sexy mood. If this happens, you may as well take a recess and kick back in front of the TV with some ice cream.

- **Taurus get-it-on song:** "Your Body Is a Wonderland," by John Mayer.
- **Taurus favorite time for amore:** two in the morning, or two in the afternoon.
- **Taurus aphrodisiac:** Gobs and gobs of money being spent on you, especially in the form of gems.

INTIMACY AND THE TAURUS MAN: Know what you're getting into—and hopefully you've got some time on your hands (or on your back, as the case may be), because this guy is insatiable. He has the sexual appetite of an adolescent trapped in a grown man's lifestyle. So if he appears to be indifferent about sex, it's likely because he's trying to hide his ravenous hunger by going the other way until he knows you're into it, too. He's a masterful and tender partner, bringing delicious dynamics to the bedroom. Though he can be traditional in his approach to lovemaking, when you're least expecting it, he'll change it up. He also appreciates when his partner has the surprises.

★ GEMINI ★

GODDESS BEHIND CLOSED DOORS: For you sex starts long before the kissing—long before the hand-holding, even. It starts with that first verbal exchange between you and your potential partner. Words are intrinsically connected to your libido. Intelligent banter is your favorite kind of foreplay. And you delight in hearing and talking about what a partner is going to do to you almost as much as you enjoy what actually happens.

Of course, there comes a time in every courtship when the best thing you can possibly do is just shut up and let it happen.

You are the sign most likely to keep a written memoir of your experiences; doing so heightens your anticipation, gets you in touch with your sexual appetite, and increases your pleasure. Of course, such a journal requires the utmost discretion and should perhaps be kept in a lockbox and buried under the floorboards.

- **Gemini get-it-on song:** "Are You Gonna Be My Girl," by Jet.
- **Gemini favorite time for amore:** any ol' time, as long as you aren't expecting it.
- **Gemini aphrodisiac:** dirty talk.

INTIMACY AND THE GEMINI MAN: Part of the fun of sex with Gemini is that you just never know when it's going to happen. Like, you could be strolling along the frozen food aisle, and Babe could meet your glance, and all of a sudden . . . well, a guy can fantasize, can't he? And Gemini's pretty darned attractive, so his optimism regarding the frequency of potential encounters is not entirely unrealistic. But don't worry, get jealous, or try to control his intimate life. He'll only resist. If you want a Gemini man all to yourself—and who wouldn't, the guy is a catch!—the law of attraction is the way to go. Focus on making your connection a scintillating thrill ride. Tickle his intellect while you tantalize his body. And once in a while, just for good measure, meet him in the frozen food section!

★ CANCER ★

GODDESS BEHIND CLOSED DOORS: Is there anything sexier than a fecund full moon? Werewolves aren't the only species that howls and growls under its primal light. As a Cancer, you not only are affected by the moon, but you can wield its power at your own will. When you're feeling amorous, it's like there's a full moon inside you that awakens your basic instincts and your partner's.

Touch is all about intimacy for you—there's nothing casual in the way you approach sex. The number one quality you desire in a partner is trustworthiness, because you will even pour your feelings into what you consider to be a strictly physical attraction. (That's how you end up falling in love with that booty-call guy, despite yourself.)

Cancer women have been known to be healed by sex—or at least by the flood of feelings that come with every real connection and act like a wonder drug, mending ailments both physical and mental.

- **Cancer get-it-on song:** "Whole Lotta Love," by Led Zeppelin.
- **Cancer favorite time for amore:** midnight.
- **Cancer aphrodisiac:** a man holding aloft a boom box in the pouring rain outside your bedroom window.

INTIMACY AND THE CANCER MAN: If you've ever fantasized about having multiple lovers over the span of, say, a month, a Cancer man can fulfill this fantasy all by himself. Because you can't be sure who you're going to get under the covers. He can be gooey sweet one time, and caveman gruff the next. He can be protective, wild, soothing, whiny, demanding, neurotic, poetic, or a mix of all of the above in a single lovemaking session. And he doesn't even know which he's going to choose, as lovemaking is an intuitive

★ SHE'S A CANCER ★

When Cancer **DEBBIE HARRY** slinked down the street circa 1973, she attracted catcalls that usually began, "Hey, blondie. . . . " So she changed the name of her band and started attracting attention from more than just construction workers and truckers. Harry's cool exterior and killer sneer make her seem untouchable and tough—but don't be fooled by that old Cancer trick. The punk icon and bottle-blond beauty is a moonchild who, like most Cancer women, has a "heart of glass." Harry's pop-art sensibilities and water-sign sensitivity culminated in off-the-charts sex appeal, while her devoted artistry was what kept her on the charts. Now she's a hall-of-famer and sometime movie star, and she's still in the flow of writing, recording, and providing platinum punk attitude for adoring fans.

expression for him. But the best part of loving a Cancer man is that he can match however you are feeling and the two of you can explore waves of emotion together—and this isn't scary for him, as it would be for many men. It's that vulnerable virility that will get you hooked on him—on all the hims he brings to the bedroom.

★ LEO ★

GODDESS BEHIND CLOSED DOORS: Have you heard about the mating practices of female lions in the wild? They damn near wear the males out, copulating once every twenty-five minutes for up to four days in a row. Yeesh. The lesson is, when a lioness is in the mood, she's *really* in the mood.

And what puts Leo in said mood faster than anything else is someone who is *way* into you. A partner who thinks that every move you make, every coy little look, every sinuous gesture, every idea that crosses your mind, is complete and utter sexy brilliance. The bedsheets are curtains to the stage of your body, and this show is definitely a thriller.

On the other hand, if a potential partner seems only marginally impressed, you have no problem canceling the performance without a moment's notice—and with no refund on the ticket. After all, sex is not a necessity for you—or at least when it is, you know that you always have an adoring partner in your own hot self.

- **Leo get-it-on song:** "Everybody Here Wants You," by Jeff Buckley.
- **Leo favorite time for amore:** before dinner. (Leo likes to be a little bit hungry and to not worry about the tummy bulge that could happen after dinner.)
- **Leo aphrodisiac:** a mirror over the bed.

INTIMACY AND THE LEO MAN: Don't let his posturing and bravado fool you—he's not conceited in bed. This guy is a giver. His primary focus is on your satisfaction. If you're cross-eyed with joy, so is he—and there is no bigger turn-on for him than the fact that he is turning you on. If you happen to be quiet and reserved when it comes to sexual expression, you're not going to receive the full benefit of a Leo man's skills. Because he feeds on his partner's response, and he only gets better when she's obviously enjoying herself. Remember, Leos need lots of encouragement, so when you tell him what a stud muffin he is, he rewards you by coming back with the sweets time and again.

★ VIRGO ★

GODDESS BEHIND CLOSED DOORS: Your sign was named for a "virgin," but not for the kind of virgin who has never had sex. In ancient Greece, the word was associated with maidens in general, even mothers, and it extolled feminine power. Still, Virgos do like to appear sexually conservative, if not downright prudish. But this is an act not to be believed for a second.

Oh, you naughty Virgos! When you delight in criticizing those whose bedroom habits don't fall within your realm of "acceptability," you actually reveal your fascination with the taboo and your secret wish to be freed from the bonds of correctness that can enslave your libido! (Which is, by the way, as healthy as a rabbit's.)

Though you are by no means easily won, you are open to a wide variety of types. You can see the sexual potential in a guy, and he often lives up to what you see in him. And because you are the one who brings out his virility in a way no other has before you, you are the kind of partner who makes an indelible impression.

- **Virgo get-it-on song:** "Samson," by Regina Spektor.
- **Virgo favorite time for amore:** after the workday, the chores, and all the business are finished.
- **Virgo aphrodisiac:** a perfectly cleared countertop. It's just begging for something to happen on top of it.

INTIMACY AND THE VIRGO MAN: He's serious about his sex. He's read about it. He's looked at the pictures and conducted his own scientific studies. No matter how experienced he actually is, he's pretty sure he knows what works, why it works, and for how long. He's generally so adept at carrying off his tricks that a gal who doesn't know any better might wonder if he's had some sort of formal training or degree to show for these skills. And because he's not afraid to follow his sexual curiosity, he tends to find sexy aspects of situations and people that would go unnoticed by the less observant. (For instance, the sexy librarian doesn't have to take off her glasses, hike up her skirt, and let down her hair for him to "get" her. She had him at "That's due on the twenty-first, sir.")

★ LIBRA ★

GODDESS BEHIND CLOSED DOORS: Like death and taxes, it's one of those inevitable human laws: Sex changes things. And Libra's answer to the whole messy conundrum of intimacy is to focus on the light and lovely aspects of getting close to another human. This Libra does with the skill of a hypnotist waving a fobbed watch in front of a subject's nose. *You are feeling sexy. . . . You are feeling veeeerrry sexy. . . .*

And though you may not admit it, or even realize it, dear Libra, you're in charge in the bedroom. You maintain your power by focusing entirely and selflessly on your partner. And with your own emotional balance still intact, your target is intoxicated by your attention, which he finds dizzying, addicting. This is how you like it.

However, as skillful as you are at keeping sex in manageable perspective and maintaining your poise, with the right person your sex strategy turns on itself, and it is you who gets hooked. The seductress is seduced by her own seduction! Suddenly, inexplicably, it has happened—you're a slave to love (cue your get-it-on song). . . .

- **Libra get-it-on song:** "Slave to Love," by Bryan Ferry.
- **Libra favorite time for amore:** when the other person is obviously frisky.
- **Libra aphrodisiac:** a well-lit room, especially in a tastefully decorated suite.

INTIMACY AND THE LIBRA MAN: He's like that adorable bloke with an accent whom all the girls would like to drag into the nearest coat closet. Except maybe he doesn't have an accent. But being a Libra guy is like its own accent—a smooth, gentlemanly tone that allows him to do any number of ungentlemanly things that no one else could possibly get away with. Oh, how he lays on the charm liberally when he wants to get to know you, and keeps on applying it all through lovemaking. He's into reciprocity, so the variety of positions and styles he employs is not so much to show off as it is to give his partner an equal opportunity for pleasure. That said, he doesn't feel he has to try hard, and he can pull off the most intricate moves with natural grace that leads you to believe it's all easy for him. Well, it is.

★ SCORPIO ★

GODDESS BEHIND CLOSED DOORS: It's just not fair. Other signs have to work to get comfortable in this delicate area of relationships. Others have to make mistakes, go through awkwardness, attain some skills, learn to trust themselves, blossom. And then there's you—born knowing how.

★ ASTROLOGICAL QUESTION ★

"In the past it's been hard for me to really open up to someone, but now I've met someone very special, an Aquarius, and I'm doing my best to trust him and not lay all the personal, intimate details of my life on him. I feel like I could really let go all the way and open up if I just knew we would be together for a long time. Do you think we will be?"

Oh, Scorpio. You like to dally with romantic notions that you belong to the person you love—that he has taken responsibility for your feelings. That once you merge into one soul, nothing can tear it asunder. This doesn't make sense to Aquarius— he can be so maddeningly, lighthearted! You're all, "I'm yours forever . . . " and he's all, "Hey, I've got tickets to the game!"

But don't lose hope, Scorpio. My advice is embrace your insecurity, accept that fact that you and this Aquarius will either be together for a few more hours or for a few more decades—what does it matter? All you have is now, anyhow. And now has always been, and continues to be, the very best time to, as you say, "let go all the way."

So you're really a dream partner, which others sense about you immediately, projecting onto you powers like those of the mythical sirens who caused sailors to crash their boats on the rocks. Your libido can be downright dangerous. Be careful where you point that thing!

Your own lack of self-consciousness allows a partner to let go of his inhibitions. And you're always operating on several levels at once. You pair your innate animalistic sense of what a partner needs in bed with a nearly psychic attunement to what he wants. Partners are particularly impressed with your nonjudgmental approach to sexual expression. Knowing that you're open-minded helps ease their fears. One might say you take the "boo" out of "taboo."

- **Scorpio get-it-on song:** "Building a Mystery," by Sarah McLachlan.
- **Scorpio favorite time for amore:** lunchtime, or any other time when most other people aren't doing it.
- **Scorpio aphrodisiac:** a scintillating confession.

INTIMACY AND THE SCORPIO MAN: It's never just sex to a Scorpio guy. He's complex and so are his desires. But don't worry, he doesn't expect you to figure him out—he doesn't even expect to figure himself out. What he does want is a partner who is along for the ride, whether it's a deep, emotional journey or a lighthearted afternoon romp. Whatever mood he's in, he's likely to be the naughtiest partner you've ever had—he's not worried about being "acceptable," and he would like it if you wouldn't worry about that, either. And he's intrigued by a woman who knows her own sexual proclivities, so that he can tune in to her needs to create a unique and fantasy-worthy experience.

★ SAGITTARIUS ★

GODDESS BEHIND CLOSED DOORS: In the comic-strip version of your sex life, the image of you would be drawn with little flames fanning out from your aura. And the last frame would be of your partner, crumpled in an exhausted heap with a blissed-out, hazy expression on his face, the caption reading, "?!?" because he has no idea what just hit him.

Passion stokes your fire; when it comes to showing your love, you are the quintessential "hottie." And after the act, you are alight with energy, ideas, and productivity. While your partner sleeps off the drug of your love, you could clean the entire house, including the inside of the refrigerator, call all of your girlfriends, find a cure for cancer, and come back ready for round two.

Always the adventurer, you are quite accepting of whatever style a partner brings to the table . . . or the shower, the kitchen sink, the airplane bathroom, the coat closet at the club, or—your last choice—the bed.

- **Sagittarius get-it-on song:** "Come Away with Me," by Norah Jones.
- **Sagittarius favorite time for amore:** when the seat belt sign below the overhead compartment has turned off.
- **Sagittarius aphrodisiac:** the scent of "strange."

INTIMACY AND THE SAGITTARIUS MAN: What do you do with a guy this intense? An unsuspecting gal might approach a Sagittarius guy in the bedroom the way an astronaut handles g-forces—by holding on tight and bearing it until there's a change in the atmosphere. But a better approach is to keep changing the "atmosphere" so that you're always keeping him a little off balance. Because he thrives on surprise, and he adores a divalicious temptress who will take charge in the bedroom.

★ℭAPRICORN★

GODDESS BEHIND CLOSED DOORS: Capricorn, have you ever been doing something mundane and entirely nonsexual when a completely unexpected, sexy, blush-inducing thought pops up in your mind, changing the rating of the whole task from G to R—or XXX—in the blink of an eye?

Chances are, the thought you had wasn't even your own—I believe this phenomenon happens when someone else is thinking naughty things about you. Because Capricorn charisma is the stuff fantasies are made of. And should one of your admirers become an actual contender for your intimate affection, this person is in for a powerful experience—as living out one's dreams tends to be.

Your famous detachment is part of what keeps lovers coming back for more. You do aloof and unattainable better than anyone, giving others the chance to strive for your affection. And you can't deny that you love the power this pattern gives you. Being able to compartmentalize your feelings is a habit that both serves and hurts you. Keep in mind that you are always at your strongest when you dare to be vulnerable.

- **Capricorn get-it-on song:** "Je T'Aime Moi Non Plus" by Serge Gainsbourg.
- **Capricorn favorite time for amore:** 10:00 PM.
- **Capricorn aphrodisiac:** a commitment.

INTIMACY AND THE CAPRICORN MAN: He wants to feel powerful in all areas of his life, and feeling powerful in the bedroom is one way to amp it up on all fronts. And it really matters to him that his partner thinks he's the be all, end all in bed. Also that she's exclusively devoted to him, and, in a very basic sense, that she's his. Of course, no one can really own another person, but he'd like it if you at least had the good manners to let him believe that during the moments of your union he is, in some profound way, inhabiting not only your body but your soul. As far as his skills go, he's earthy and sensual, but if left to his own devices, he can be too controlled. So he needs to be with a woman who understands that the tango of sex is a push/pull dance, made more exciting when each partner takes turns playing with elements of tension, tenderness, strength, and submission.

★ AQUARIUS ★

GODDESS BEHIND CLOSED DOORS: The person who coined the term "friends with benefits" just had to be an Aquarius. You also invented "sexual stand-up" (being funny between the sheets), sex toys (especially ones that light up), and the popular phrase "Relax, it's just sex." With levity as your guiding principle in all things sexual and un, you often wonder what everyone else seems to be so uptight about.

But when it comes to your sexual attitudes, by no means does "easy-breezy" translate into "sleazy." You're actually super choosy about whom you allow into the inner sanctum of your intimate life. Ideally, this is someone who is mature enough to behave as a gentleman, a man, a mensch, no matter how intense the physical connection gets. Because you can't stand it when sex causes people to lose their heads and passion causes people to act like idiots. You're not one to plan a seduction. Sex happens. And that's how you like it—spontaneous, free-flowing, and fun. And if it ceases being that way, you cease being interested in it. So you need a partner who can change it up, keep it fresh, and stay in the moment with you.

- **Aquarian get-it-on song:** "Say It Right," by Nelly Furtado.
- **Aquarius favorite time for amore:** after a party. Or during one.
- **Aquarian aphrodisiac:** Sexy literature is the key that unlocks your libido.

INTIMACY AND THE AQUARIUS MAN: Millions of dollars in psychotherapy fees have been racked up by women in relationships with Aquarius guys. The billable minutes tick away while these poor chicks ponder, Does he want me? Or is he merely teasing me to see if I want him? And what is my next move? His casual attitude about romance is teamed with brilliant banter, so the experience of dating him is like being caught in some kind of Aaron Sorkin series—a lot of walking and talking, but when is someone going to take off their clothes? And the answer is: when you take off your clothes. Really. Don't wait for something to happen—you'll be waiting forever. Just take off your clothes. Turn off your head and he'll turn off his. Use your lips for something other than making words. There, I've just saved you hundreds of dollars—now you can rant to your therapist about something else.

★ PISCES ★

PISCES GODDESS BEHIND CLOSED DOORS: There's an invisible circle around Pisces women—an extended bubble, a secret dimension that only Pisces is aware of, if she even is. And those who are able to get inside this bubble find that the world there is not like the world outside, but like a heightened version of it. The colors are more vivid. The sounds are dreamier. And time passes not like the tick of a clock, but like the inconsistent flow of a river. Sometimes moments rush, sometimes they trickle, and one can always feel the wet seconds as they slip by. Such is the poetic intimacy of Pisces.

How do you do this, Pisces? Do you cast a spell? Do you somehow seduce potential loves with the heady elixir of your romantic will? Do you use smoke and mirrors to entice them into your magic trick? *Naw.* Go on, shrug your shoulders. You don't even know what you're doing. You have no idea what effect you create. You're just flirting and it, as they say, "ain't no thing."

But it is something. It's a spiritual intention you set, either consciously or unconsciously, to turn your intimate union with others into a sacred act. The attention you give your love life makes it so. Anyone whô is lucky enough to know you in this way is moved by the experience.

- **Pisces get-it-on song:** "Spirit," by Van Morrison.
- **Pisces favorite time for amore:** during a spiritual awakening.
- **Pisces aphrodisiac:** whispered existential conversation.

INTIMACY AND THE PISCES MAN: If you, like Marvin Gaye, sometimes get the feeling that you need sexual healing, Pisces is the man for the job. He's the love doctor who takes a holistic approach—the guy can give a full-body massage to your soul. But don't ask him how he does it. It's so natural, he's probably not even aware of his talent—he just assumes that every guy is as powerful as he is at moving women between the sheets. He may not be the type to even know what your "chi" is, but he can raise it nonetheless with his attention to your subtle womanly needs. He doesn't want to have sex with you, he wants to awaken your spirit. Okay, maybe he does want to have sex with you, but awakening your spirit is a happy by-product of the union.

goodwill among goddesses

FRIENDS

Friendships between women are unique—even on a chemical level. Researchers at UCLA did a study that suggested that female bonding produces stress-relieving oxytocin in the brain. And the more a woman does what these scientists call "tending and befriending," the calmer she feels and the healthier she becomes. Furthermore, friendship ties have been credited with lowering blood pressure, heart rate, and cholesterol. And a Harvard Medical School study concluded that a lack of friendly support is as detrimental to health as smoking or being overweight. So the moral of the story is . . .

Friendships are wonderful—they really are! And that's what I was trying to tell my friend Sophie the other day when she was griping about a mutual pal who, in Sophie's words, "is being completely self-absorbed." The evidence: two lunch dates canceled at the last minute, a thoughtless comment about Sophie's boyfriend, a failure to pay her share of that shower gift we all went in on. . . . The list yammered on.

I've learned that one must be extremely careful about what one says in this type of conversation, because one never knows what form the words will take in someone else's mouth. Girlfriends armed with what the other girl said can cause serious wounds to everyone involved. So I mumbled something about our pal going through her Saturn return—an astrological phenomenon that occurs between ages twenty-eight and thirty and involves soul-searching lessons—and *maybe she needs us to cut her a little slack*. But even as I spoke the words, I knew that wasn't the full deal. Actually, our pal had complained to me about Sophie as well—these two could push each other's buttons like a telephone banking session—*beep, beep, bop, bleep, bloop*—beeatch! Why couldn't they just get along?

Upon further consideration, I wondered if what all my friends needed to coincide harmoniously was a lesson in the other's friendship style. For instance, if our pal understood that Sophie, who happens to be a sensitive Scorpio, holds one-on-one time sacred, maybe she would think twice before canceling the lunch date. And if Sophie understood that our pal is a busy Gemini who probably doesn't even remember that she never put in for the shower gift and only needs a gentle reminder, maybe she wouldn't be personally offended.

A specific friendship talent is mapped into every person's stars. Some signs, like Aquarius and Sagittarius, are adept at throwing big, raucous parties. Libra is an expert matchmaker for her friends, who will find their lives totally enriched by the introductions she makes. Capricorns can keep in touch with a person for a lifetime. For those who haven't tapped into their friendship talent yet, I guarantee that doing so is not only a fabulously rewarding experience, but also a way to steer clear of small-minded problems by living and loving bigger.

Knowing our friends' social operating systems helps us be more compassionate, less petty, and better able to spend our "tending and befriending" time in mutually nurturing ways. Why should we merely "get by" with a little help from our friends, when we can soar above mundane life on our laughter, fun, glamour, joy, and good ol' health-producing oxytocin—in other words, "get high" with a little help from our friends?

★ ARIES ★

FRIENDSHIP STYLE: She's that girl who, in the second grade, wanted to be sure that you were best friends forever. And when you said that Sally was also your best friend, she said that was impossible because you could only have one best friend, and then she beat up Sally. She's all grown up now and much more diplomatic, but she still wants to know she has a special place in your heart.

FRIENDSHIP TALENT: motivation. If you tell her you want something, you'd better be serious, because she's ruthlessly supportive. She'll cheer from the sidelines. She'll buckle a jet pack to your back. She'll help you find incentives and create deadlines—and if those don't work, she'll threaten you.

YOU'RE ESPECIALLY GLAD SHE'S YOUR FRIEND WHEN: you're in transition between jobs, homes, men, and life stages. She has incredible mojo when it comes to finding fresh opportunities, and she's fearless about getting started. This rubs off on you. Let her take your hand and lead you in jumping off of the high dive of life into the pool of new beginnings.

GIRLFRIEND ACTIVITY NOT TO MISS: Attending competitions together. It's fun to get all riled up rooting for your team or contestant. Victories somehow feel more victorious with her around, and defeats only make the next victory sweeter.

HER BITCHINESS COMES OUT WHEN: she thinks you like someone else better. Make sure she feels special. And never give her the same gift you gave someone else.

WHEN THINGS GET HAIRY, THE BEST WAY TO SMOOTH IT OVER IS: to surrender. Sometimes it's just better to let her be right and move on.

SHOW HER YOU CARE BY: rallying behind her with unconditional support. Though she appears to be unflappably confident, she still needs to know that her pals believe in her. So when she says, "I'm quitting my job to join the Peace Corps" or, "I'm breaking up with this guy" or, "I'm leasing a Porsche," don't come up with a bunch of questions about her choice or play devil's advocate. She's not the type who needs someone to find the weaknesses in a plan. Just say, "Fab!" and tell her how her myriad talents will shine through the endeavor.

★ 𝕿AURUS ★

FRIENDSHIP STYLE: She's the true-blue, lifelong friend. She's still there even when you don't go to the same school anymore, are no longer in contact with the person who introduced you to each other, and have moved to a different state. And no matter how much time passes between your phone calls, it's like you never missed a beat—her authenticity enables you to find common ground immediately.

FRIENDSHIP TALENT: enjoyment. Her belief is that life is rich, it's beautiful, it's delicious. And because she sees the "yummy," she helps you see it—and taste, feel, hear, and smell it.

YOU'RE ESPECIALLY GLAD SHE'S YOUR FRIEND WHEN: you need to relax. She's a relaxation pro—okay, so maybe she doesn't exactly get paid to relax, but if there were such a job, she'd be the president of the company.

GIRLFRIEND ACTIVITY NOT TO MISS: dinners. Long, decadent dinners with drinks and appetizers and several selections from the dessert tray to sample . . . and the riveting "dishing" that goes along with the eating makes the whole experience divine.

HER BITCHINESS COMES OUT WHEN: you borrow her stuff. In fact, maybe it's better just not to.

WHEN THINGS GET HAIRY, THE BEST WAY TO SMOOTH IT OVER IS: to give her space. Let her work things out in her own good time. Explanations and apologies don't go over well unless they are brief, believable, and well timed.

SHOW HER YOU CARE BY: buying her a nifty gifty. You can't go wrong by plunking down some change for the status symbols she might be hesitant to buy herself—but oh, does she want them. Paying extra for a well-known, high-end label is never a bad idea where Taurus is concerned, because she eagerly appreciates both the quality and the thought that went into your choice.

★ GEMINI ★

FRIENDSHIP STYLE: She likes to have a zillion of them. Which means she has only 10.5 minutes a year to devote to each one, which is of course just ridiculous. So she relegates her outermost circle to a few seconds a year in order to give the inner circle a few hours. Her other friendship strategy is multitasking—which is why you've probably done laundry and/or grocery shopped with her on more than one occasion. Periodically she throws a humongous party or two so she can mingle, schmooze, and make it up to anyone who feels neglected. And she's such a groovy chick that if she's spending any one-on-one time at all with you, you feel pretty honored.

FRIENDSHIP TALENT: being hip. She's all over the latest and greatest people, hot topics, career tips, dating "dos," trendy places, beauty tips . . . you name it, she has an opinion and a hookup for you.

YOU'RE ESPECIALLY GLAD SHE'S YOUR FRIEND WHEN: you feel blasé. Because no one can spit-shine a lackluster day like your gabby Gemini gal pal. With every conversation, your day gets brighter.

★ SHE'S A GEMINI ★

What you oughta know about **ALANIS MORISSETTE** is that she's not only a Gemini twin, she's also an actual twin. She and her twin brother, Wade, were born in Ottawa, Canada, at a time when Mercury, Mars, and Saturn were all in emotional Cancer. Since then, Morissette has been a child star, a teen star, and a multiplatinum, Grammy-winning pop star. She's played God in the movies and Lolita in her songs. She's done Catholicism, Buddhism, and *The Vagina Monologues* (which, according to one of her songs, isn't nearly the naughtiest thing she's performed in a theater). Geminis get their rock on by staying in motion, seeking fresh knowledge, finding new reasons to howl, and taking long breaks between each reinvention of themselves.

GIRLFRIEND ACTIVITY NOT TO MISS: shopping. You're not going to spend as much as you would shopping with other signs, and you're going to get only the hottest items, because there's no way she's letting you buy anything but must-haves.

HER BITCHINESS COMES OUT WHEN: you blatantly copy her. She's always happy to advise you, and is flattered when you use her suggestions. But if you ever imitate her without giving her credit, or without her knowing your plan, she won't take it as a compliment. She puts many hours and brain waves into her style picks and wants to know that you can appreciate her effort.

WHEN THINGS GET HAIRY, THE BEST WAY TO SMOOTH IT OVER IS: to blow it off. "Easy breezy" is her friendship motto. When you keep it light, she may just forget all about whatever has come between you.

SHOW HER YOU CARE BY: doing the unexpected, especially when she's blue. Bringing her matinee tickets on a dreary Sunday. Stopping by with brownies when you know she's having boy trouble. Surprises delight her and return her to her usually buoyant self.

★ CANCER ★

FRIENDSHIP STYLE: She's a sweetheart who accepts you as you are. She really tries not to judge you, and she doesn't put limits on her friendship. Furthermore, she considers it an honor to celebrate all your major life events in a big way, even if you don't want to. She's the type who would throw you a baby shower for your third kid, or a "virgin"-themed bachelor-ette party for your third wedding.

FRIENDSHIP TALENT: coaching. She's psychic when it comes to what you should do next. And her ability to steer you toward a powerful long-term goal is downright uncanny. For this reason, you never mind when she says, "I told you so," because she indeed did—and she was so right.

YOU'RE ESPECIALLY GLAD SHE'S YOUR FRIEND WHEN: you've messed up big time. Put it this way: If you're ever arrested, your one phone call would not be wasted on her.

GIRLFRIEND ACTIVITY NOT TO MISS: slumber parties! She's the consum-mate hostess for this kind of soiree. It's like being back in the third grade, except the Oreos come with wine instead of milk, and the 3:00 AM conver-sation is about topics ever so much more interesting than who ate glue this week at school.

HER BITCHINESS COMES OUT WHEN: you betray her confidence. If she says, "This is just between you and me," do not forget it. And if you do forget it, do not confess!

WHEN THINGS GET HAIRY, THE BEST WAY TO SMOOTH IT OVER IS: to run for cover. Seriously, you won't like her when she's mad. Then, when it appears that the steam has stopped escaping from her ears, emerge with your head bowed, apologize profusely, and get the hell out. Wait a couple days before calling her again.

SHOW HER YOU CARE BY: professing your love. She'll pretend like she hates it when you're mushy and sentimental—she'll crack jokes and deflect your compliments—but secretly she longs to hear sweet words of support and admiration from her closest buds.

 ★ **LEO** ★

FRIENDSHIP STYLE: If you lose track of her, just follow the sounds of laughter and applause. She's living life at the center of a follow spot, and sometimes you wonder if she considers you to be more of a pal, or a fan— either way, she's a good one to have on your side. She's the friend who bridges the gap between your work friends and your childhood friends, your gym friends and your neighborhood friends—she's the one who can talk to anyone and entertain everyone. She's generous and loving, but she also requires validation and acknowledgment in order to stay that way.

FRIENDSHIP TALENT: speaking well of you. Whether she's giving a toast at your wedding or a letter of reference for a job, or just telling everyone she knows that you make a killer frittata, her words paint you in a beautiful light.

YOU'RE ESPECIALLY GLAD SHE'S YOUR FRIEND WHEN: you have a nerve-racking event to go to, especially where you'll need to mingle with power players. She doesn't use icebreakers; she *is* the icebreaker.

GIRLFRIEND ACTIVITY NOT TO MISS: The after-party discussion. Her retelling of your shared experience is so vivid, informed, and interesting that it teaches you to see things in a way that increases your enjoyment of the event.

HER BITCHINESS COMES OUT WHEN: you take her for granted. A well-timed thank-you note will usually calm the lioness.

WHEN THINGS GET HAIRY, THE BEST WAY TO SMOOTH IT OVER IS: to work it out in real time. If you leave the situation unresolved, she'll have time to put that limitless imagination to work—avoid this likelihood at all costs. You do not want that imagination unleashed against you!

SHOW HER YOU CARE BY: laughing with her. She's on top of the world when she feels she's amusing you. Tell her how clever she is. Go to her "show," whatever that may be—she's always up to something!

★ 𝕭𝕴𝕽𝕲𝕺 ★

FRIENDSHIP STYLE: If there's one sign that every woman absolutely must have in her pantheon of girlfriends, it's Virgo. Gal-pal relationships are her forte. She's conscientious. She's dependable. She remembers all the big and little things about you—that you've never had the chicken pox, the age you were when your parents got divorced, and that you dated a "Dave" for five minutes. And when you think you've bored her to death with a story or one of your issues, she's eager to hear more—she's genuinely interested.

FRIENDSHIP TALENT: saving you from looking bad. She always knows what's appropriate. If in doubt, just ask her what shoes to wear, what to say, and how best to say it. She will not steer you wrong.

YOU'RE ESPECIALLY GLAD SHE'S YOUR FRIEND WHEN: it's time to celebrate you. She does it right. Her love is a very specific kind of attention, and she can make you feel rich for having it.

GIRLFRIEND ACTIVITY TO NOT MISS: working together. Whether you're helping a mutual friend move, raising money for charity, or actually doing business, her work ethic and ideas are sure to inspire.

HER BITCHINESS COMES OUT WHEN: she disapproves. She's quick to take the moral high ground—mostly because she lives there. And she has a hard time hiding it when she doesn't like what you say or what you're up to.

WHEN THINGS GET HAIRY, THE BEST WAY TO SMOOTH IT OVER IS: to validate her. Assure her that even though you may not agree with her, you appreciate her attention, her input, and the fact that she cares so deeply about you.

SHOW HER YOU CARE BY: returning some of the very specific attention she lavishes on you. Love is in the details.

★ LIBRA ★

FRIENDSHIP STYLE: She's the glue that holds any social scene together. It's not necessarily because she throws parties or constructs a busy social schedule. It's because she fits into and legitimates any situation she's part of with her supreme diplomacy and gorgeous manners. She makes casual get-togethers seem meaningful. She honors even your most whimsical, impractical, or plain bad ideas with honest consideration. And she is a master of the ancient and dying art called "listening."

FRIENDSHIP TALENT: classing it up. A barbeque on the porch? She arrives and suddenly it's "dining alfresco." Outfit not working? She'll give you her scarf, and magically you're fashionably eclectic. Boyfriend awkward? She'll ask him the questions that make him seem adorably bumbling and Hugh Grant–esque.

YOU'RE ESPECIALLY GLAD SHE'S YOUR FRIEND WHEN: no one is getting along. She knows better than to take sides.

GIRLFRIEND ACTIVITY NOT TO MISS: voting. Is voting a sport? She certainly approaches it that way. And if you're apathetic, she'll talk you through the pros and cons until ballot initiative 19 actually seems interesting to you.

HER BITCHINESS COMES OUT WHEN: she feels pressured. She needs to make decisions in her own time, and she doesn't want anyone crowding her process.

WHEN THINGS GET HAIRY, THE BEST WAY TO SMOOTH IT OVER IS: to agree. Who cares that you don't agree? She's used to doing all the agreeing—she likes agreeing—and it's very agreeable that someone else would do the agreeing for a change. Agreed?

SHOW HER YOU CARE BY: indulging her softness for flowers, fads, and other lovely things that will quickly fade. The brevity of beauty makes it all the more important to behold. There's no such thing as frivolity in Libra's world. There are only pretty things and ugly things.

★ SCORPIO ★

FRIENDSHIP STYLE: She doesn't let just anyone be her friend. Her inner circle comprises a select and cherished few. Sure, she may appear to have a vast network of platonic ties, but there is a distinct difference for the serious Scorpio between friends and acquaintances. Friendship is a sacred bond. Also note that it's a subtle kind of love she gives to her gal pals. You may not even realize the deep, abiding affection she has for you, and then one day she surprises you with an acknowledgment that moves you to the core.

FRIENDSHIP TALENT: discretion. Remember those photos of the Loch Ness Monster, and how a friend of the photographer allegedly claimed on his deathbed that the whole thing was a hoax? Well, a Scorpio girlfriend would *never* have done that. She would have gone to the grave with the story you agreed upon. In a dying gasp, she would mutter, "That sea monster . . . " (sputter, choke) " . . . was sooooo *big*. . . . " (kerplunk, flatline).

YOU'RE ESPECIALLY GLAD SHE'S YOUR FRIEND WHEN: you don't know where to bury the body. Okay, maybe that's a little extreme, but we've all done passionate, selfish, or thoughtless things that in more lucid moments we rather wish we hadn't. Your Scorpio friend is not only forgiving in these cases, she almost makes it seem as though Mother Teresa would have done the same thing in your circumstance—and she definitely helps you resolve what you must in order to move on.

GIRLFRIEND ACTIVITY NOT TO MISS: trolling for guys. For her, meeting men is a game—a game she's won many times. So she has fun with the whole scene—she's downright hilarious at times—and her confidence attracts exciting and interesting prospects for the both of you.

HER BITCHINESS COMES OUT WHEN: she decides it's time to be a bitch. See, she's not afraid of being a bitch, she doesn't see a thing wrong with it, and she can turn her inner bitch on or off whenever it suits her. So you shouldn't be afraid, either. Just expect that it's part of the complex and wonderful Scorpio-girlfriend package.

WHEN THINGS GET HAIRY, THE BEST WAY TO SMOOTH IT OVER IS: with a hug. For all her flinty, edgy moodiness, what she really craves is intimacy. Tons of it. Pushing you away is usually just a test, and a signal that you should come closer.

SHOW HER YOU CARE BY: making sure you spend plenty of one-on-one time with her. You don't have to go anywhere, either. Some of the best times you'll ever have together are at her place, just chillin'.

★ SAGITTARIUS ★

FRIENDSHIP STYLE: Being in her circle of friends is like being a member of the United Nations. The main thing you have in common with her other friends is that you both live on Planet Earth. Other than that, many different languages, vocations, generations, and orientations are represented in her fabulous posse. And you're lucky to be included. If you're at all lacking in platonic variety, one Sagittarius girlfriend is all you need to color your world.

FRIENDSHIP TALENT: tolerance. It's this underappreciated virtue that, if applied globally, could heal the world. But when applied personally, it's simply a pleasure to hang with her. Because you can be who you are and it's okay. There is no loneliness when you reach out to someone who has the capacity to appreciate you "as is."

YOU'RE ESPECIALLY GLAD SHE'S YOUR FRIEND WHEN: you have a few days off from work and a vehicle. She's the consummate road warrior. And if you have a few weeks off and a passport, all the better!

GIRLFRIEND ACTIVITY NOT TO MISS: air travel. You really haven't flown until you've flown next to a Sagittarius gal. You don't need first-class tickets, because she knows how to get the flight attendant to slip you all the free extras, and she makes sure that if there's an open seat to be had, it's in your aisle so you can stretch your legs out. The whole flight is a party, as you talk about all the fun things you're going to do when you get "there."

HER BITCHINESS COMES OUT WHEN: you get clingy. And her definition of clingy is requiring any commitment at all. Asking her to be on time to the matinee, for instance, is tantamount to asking her to name her firstborn after you. The girl doesn't like to be obligated in any way. Period.

WHEN THINGS GET HAIRY, THE BEST WAY TO SMOOTH IT OVER IS: with a change of scenery. If you disagree in the car, then just get out and jog around the park. Things will look different to her from there. And if you disagree at the park, walk into the mall. It's a whole new scene in there.

SHOW HER YOU CARE BY: giving her lots of leeway. So what if she forgets to call on your birthday? She'll make up for it with an exotic present. And if you don't talk to her for a few weeks, that's fine—when you do see her, you may just spend the whole weekend together, backpacking through your nearest national park. Think "big picture," and you'll never be disappointed.

★ CAPRICORN ★

FRIENDSHIP STYLE: She makes you feel like a VIP, but don't give her too much credit for this. You see, if you're Capricorn's friend, there's a good chance you actually *are* a VIP. She doesn't see the point in hanging out with people who don't have more to offer than just company. In her mind, friends should be both fun and useful (even if their main use is being fun). She tries not to be a snob, but the fact is, she'd rather stay home than hang out with ordinary folk. So if she's hanging out with you, it means you rate big-time.

FRIENDSHIP TALENT: rocking your world. Need an apartment? She knows the manager of the building. Need a formal dress? She'll introduce you to the designer. Whatever it is you want, she has the hookup—and she plays in the big leagues, so prepare to be not only fulfilled, but transformed.

YOU'RE ESPECIALLY GLAD SHE'S YOUR FRIEND WHEN: you're unemployed. A few phone calls are all it takes to get doors swinging open— yeah, of course she knows the CEO. She probably *is* the CEO.

★ COCKTAIL HOUR ★

DRINK SPECIALS AT CLUB ARIES

Spicy Bloody Mary (Because you like it hot.)

Sazerac (Rumored to be the first cocktail.)

Gin and Cherry Sling (Red and zesty.)

DRINK SPECIALS AT CLUB TAURUS

Butterscotch Delight (Sooo decadent . . .)

Premium Scotch on the rocks (The pricier, the better.)

Chocolate Mintini (Chocolate and mint. Two birds, one glass.)

DRINK SPECIALS AT CLUB GEMINI

Grasshopper (Your sign rules the insect.)

Pomtini (Because you're trendy that way.)

Jack Daniel's (For your bad twin.)

DRINK SPECIALS AT CLUB CANCER

Moonshot (Why, of course!)

Sea Breeze (Shaken, not blended, for when you're feeling same.)

Pint of cider (At the pub, with friends.)

continued...

DRINK SPECIALS AT CLUB LEO

White Lion (Duh!)

Melon Dramatic (Double duh!)

Sunburst (With two straws, and tip your glass to your cosmic ruler.)

DRINK SPECIALS AT CLUB VIRGO

Manhattan (A refined classic, like you.)

Champagne spritzer (The drink of supermodels, Virgos, and Virgo supermodels.)

Sex on the Beach (As the sign of the virgin, you sound extra dirty ordering it.)

DRINK SPECIALS AT CLUB LIBRA

Venus (And don't forget to toast your ruling planet.)

Pinot noir (The stuff of romance.)

Margarita (Blended, with salt. It's sweet, sour, and salty all at once, just like you!)

DRINK SPECIALS AT CLUB SCORPIO

Scorpion (One is enough, Scorp. This one packs a sting!)

Secret (For when you're working your mystique.)

Shot of premium tequila (Straight up, like you.)

DRINK SPECIALS AT CLUB SAGITTARIUS

Flaming Hot Buttered Rum (It's on fire–so are you.)
Jupiter Cocktail (With a wink to your Big Planet Daddy.)
Bahama Mama (Don't you wish you were there now?)

DRINK SPECIALS AT CLUB CAPRICORN

Godmother (Sip while pontificating in a raspy voice.)
Dirty Martini (Straight up, extra olives–so VIP.)
Old-Fashioned (Classic as a Cole Porter song.)

DRINK SPECIALS AT CLUB AQUARIUS

Disco Fizz (Sip between stints on the dance floor
doing the hustle.)
Purple Rain (How unusual!)
Beer (For the casual hang.)

DRINK SPECIALS AT CLUB PISCES

Gloom Lifter (When you're in a mood. You know what
I'm talkin' about.)
California merlot (Classically complex.)
Pink Mermaid (Creamy and dreamy for Neptune's daughter.)

GIRLFRIEND ACTIVITY NOT TO MISS: networking. She does conventions, seminars, and industry dinners like children do trick-or-treating. The two of you get all dressed up and work the room, collecting goodies in the form of opportunities, contacts, or actual goodies from everyone you talk to.

HER BITCHINESS COMES OUT WHEN: you lose your manners. She's way into etiquette. If you don't follow the rules, she takes it as a personal sign of disrespect.

WHEN THINGS GET HAIRY, THE BEST WAY TO SMOOTH IT OVER IS: with a formal, preferably public, apology, followed by a "please forgive me" note, followed by a thank-you note when she finally does forgive you.

SHOW HER YOU CARE BY: supporting her in achieving her goals. She appears to be self-motivated and driven, but she longs to get her props as much as the next type A personality. So compliment her, celebrate her, and even flatter her—you can't pour it on too thick. When she's weary (and you'll never guess this by looking at her, but she does get weary!), your sweet encouragement will carry her through.

★ AQUARIUS ★

FRIENDSHIP STYLE: To Aquarius, there are only two types of people: those who are her friends, and those who will someday be her friends. Lovers are friends with benefits. Enemies are friends with detriments. People who have sued her are friends with settlements. As far as Aquarius is concerned, the commonalities between earthlings are grounds enough for fellowship. What does this mean if she's your best friend? Only that you're sharing her with the whole world—so hopefully you can fit a lot of people into your car.

FRIENDSHIP TALENT: seeing your magnificence. When you've lost track of what's special about you, or what you have to offer, or indeed who you are, she'll remind you.

YOU'RE ESPECIALLY GLAD SHE'S YOUR FRIEND WHEN: your faith in humanity has been shaken. She'll remind you of all that's decent, lovable, and super fun about the human race—and she'll probably do this while dancing.

GIRLFRIEND ACTIVITY NOT TO MISS: dancing. She's doesn't care that she's the only one on the dance floor, or that there is no dance floor, or that there is no music. Join her in her groovy revelry, and you too will be liberated from the mental prison of *What are they thinking about me?*

HER BITCHINESS COMES OUT WHEN: you don't recycle. And don't even bring up the topic of global warming. In fact, maybe it's better to not talk politics at all with her.

WHEN THINGS GET HAIRY, THE BEST WAY TO SMOOTH IT OVER IS: to give it a good night's rest. She'll probably forget about it by tomorrow. And if she doesn't, then you should act like you have and she'll likely follow suit.

SHOW HER YOU CARE BY: giving to her favorite cause, sponsoring her in the triathlon, or joining her in the protest line.

★ PISCES ★

FRIENDSHIP STYLE: Like the wizened sensei in a Hong Kong martial arts film, she's in no hurry to make new friends. So don't be surprised if, the first time you attempt to connect with her, you get the distinct feeling that she'd rather direct her attention to something much more important—for instance, catching flies with chopsticks—than giving you the time of day. This habit is not to be taken personally, however; in the case of both the cinematic sensei and the Pisces gal, it's a technique used to weed out the weak. If you persist, her inner circle, which is like a private sect with secret knowledge and elite privileges, will warm to you. Once you're on the inside, you're sisters. Know that the bond is sacred to her, and that she would karate-chop a ninja in half to protect it.

FRIENDSHIP TALENT: empathy. When you're elated, you'll have to pull her off the ceiling. When you're down, she's in the depths right there with you. It's as though she really feels whatever you're going through—and the truth is, she does feel it. And she can help you heal it.

YOU'RE ESPECIALLY GLAD SHE'S YOUR FRIEND WHEN: life gets one-dimensional. She's deep. She sees layers of meaning inside layers of meaning. And when you're with her you can become awestruck by simple miracles—like a leaf dancing in the wind, or a BCBG sweater that's marked down 50 percent.

GIRLFRIEND ACTIVITY NOT TO MISS: emptying your mind of negativity (or of everything). Yoga, jogging, meditating, singing in the choir, gardening, humming, driving, stretching, tanning, pedicuring . . . anything at all-ing in her company turns into a Zen retreat.

HER BITCHINESS COMES OUT WHEN: you hurt her feelings. How did you hurt them this time? Was it something you said, did, forgot, remembered? See, that's the thing. It's so easy to set her off, who knows? She's sensitive—overly sensitive, many would say. So when her bitchiness comes out, just roll your eyes (but for God's sake, not in front of her!) and bless her in your mind, as you refuse to engage in the drama.

WHEN THINGS GET HAIRY, THE BEST WAY TO SMOOTH IT OVER IS: with kid gloves and on tiptoes, lest you crack one of the eggshells you'll be walking on until the whole thing blows over.

SHOW HER YOU CARE BY: making her a mix CD. She adores music and finds herself in every song. Adding to the soundtrack to her life is one way to recognize the rare, unique, tenderhearted, talented woman she is.

theory of relativity

FAMILY

I like to think of family relationships as mandatory friendships—friendships you make with people whom you may, on the surface, not have so much in common with. Except, perhaps, that you have spent most of your lives together. And share DNA. And, in all probability, even smell alike. You know, people you have nothing in common with, except everything.

That's what makes the family dynamic so weird and poignant and profound. As fantastic and horrible as things get in families, you're pretty much stuck with each other. And as every teenager who has wanted to blow off the family dinner to go hang out with friends can attest, blood, though it is thicker than water, is generally not as fun to drink or swim in.

Yet when you make friends with your family, you establish the most powerful and important friendship of your life. Being at peace with family can mean being at peace with yourself. For some of us, it's hard to feel whole if we don't have a solid connection to our "peeps." Or, if not exactly a solid connection, at least one that allows you to get along when you're all forced into a room together, which inevitably happens in families.

Sometimes getting along is just a matter of accepting how the other person likes to communicate with their next of kin, and being aware of your own communication comfort zone for relatives. The stars provide you with sparkling clues and let you in on where the boundaries fall in these intimate relationships—because making up with an Aries sibling after an argument is not the same as working things through with an Aquarius. Expecting these differences can help you be more thoughtful as you cater your approach. Read on to learn what your family really thinks about you, how to best deal with them during the holidays, and more star-studded advice to help you bring a little peace, love, and understanding to your family tree.

★ ARIES ★

COMMUNICATING: You're frequently the first to offer help, an invitation, or a phone call. You're the first to visit family that's out of town, or have a big celebration dinner at your place. Sometimes it's frustrating to you when you seem to be the only one initiating family contact—does this mean they don't care as much about you as you do them? No, no, it's nothing like that. Your love is definitely reciprocated full strength. It's just that others get used to your starting the ball rolling, and you do it so well that they figure you prefer things this way. Your ideas are fun, and you make it easy for others to join in the action. So they'll let you lead until you ask someone else to step in.

HOW THEY SEE YOU: as their right to brag. You make 'em proud. You've done it from the start—your birth was a highlight of your family's story, and your legend continues. Family members love to boast about your accomplishments behind your back. They feel powerful by association when others are impressed.

HOW YOU WANT THEM TO SEE YOU: as someone who needs a hug. Heck, most times you could use twenty hugs. Though you can come across as a tough and independent chick, you require as much tenderness as the next gal. Take periodic breaks from being the strong one.

WHAT THEY LOVE ABOUT YOU (whether they tell you or not): your gusto. You don't do anything halfway, and this always makes for dynamic results.

WHAT DRIVES YOU NUTS ABOUT THEM: They take so long to make group decisions. It would be so much simpler if they would just let you decide for them. There would be a lot less waffling and a lot more doing.

HOLIDAY COPING STRATEGY: While I would advise many signs to be more assertive and honest with family, I find that Aries is usually already more honest and assertive than necessary. I say, lie and defer. Try gentle. Try nonconfrontational. Try a little flattery and sweetness before you duck out. It's going to feel weird at first, but you'll be surprised by how much energy you conserve by not going "there" (and I think you know what I mean by "there," Aries—the place where you are standing when everything starts catching on fire). I mean, really, is it that important that your opinion be asserted in situations that typically only come up once a year?

STELLAR FAMILY ACTIVITIES: sports—especially football and softball, biking, flying kites, picnicking, starting businesses together, chess, talking around the kitchen table (especially in the morning).

Aries mothers are: **spunky**
Aries daughters are: **strong-willed**
Aries sisters are: **bold**
Aries wives are: **passionate**

★ TAURUS ★

COMMUNICATING: A recent UCLA study determined that 93 percent of communication effectiveness is based on interpreting nonverbal cues. I believe that had the study been conducted among only Taurus chicks and their family members, the percentage would have gone up to 98. Because a Taurus woman doesn't need to open her mouth or her ears to know that her mom is in a bad mood, her kid is hiding something, or her bro is about to hit her up for twenty bucks. Taurus women can sum up the family scene in one glance, even before the first sip of morning coffee. In fact, if you're a Taurus woman, you probably prefer to get your information in this quiet way, especially in the morning.

HOW THEY SEE YOU: as Stable Mabel. (You know her—she's the cousin of Even Steven.) The go-to gal, the rock of the family—if rocks had credit cards, that is. They know they can count on you for a variety of needs, from baby-sitting to driving to emotional-problem-solving to borrowing money. (Okay, maybe you get the last request more than you do the other ones.)

HOW YOU WANT THEM TO SEE YOU: You wish they were slightly afraid of you. Though you like to be included, there are times when you *really* need to be alone in your own space. And inevitably, others breach that boundary. Not interrupting you and not crowding you are signs of respect—and practices you wish they'd employ more often.

WHAT THEY LOVE ABOUT YOU (whether they tell you or not): your faithfulness. It can be a fast-paced, hyped-out, negative-slanted world out there, and everyone needs a solid place where they can land and catch a breath. You provide that place. It's in your presence. And during those times when everything is changing quickly, in weird ways, your constancy is a surprise.

WHAT DRIVES YOU NUTS ABOUT THEM: They need to learn to chill. You can't stand it when drama escalates over nothing. Calm and steady wins the race, and it also wins whatever ridiculous argument is going on and stirring up the family dynamic.

HOLIDAY COPING STRATEGY: Know what's going on, or not going on, and then relax. When things get hectic and many different people and personalities are involved, adhering to a schedule, or at least to an order of events, helps you maintain your sanity. At the same time, don't expect others to keep to the plan—that expectation will cause you stress. Being aware of the plan keeps you in your "chill zone." If there is no plan, know that, so that you can settle into the fact that nothing is going on.

STELLAR FAMILY ACTIVITIES: walking, singing, dining, shopping, playing games, camping.

Taurus mothers are: **sweet**
Taurus daughters are: **abiding**
Taurus sisters are: **good humored**
Taurus wives are: **faithful**

★ GEMINI ★

COMMUNICATING: There's a theory that families are only as healthy as their communication lines are open. Gemini subscribes wholly to this theory and makes it her personal mission to check her connection, in the manner of a Verizon test man riding a donkey through the desert and proclaiming, "Can you hear me now?" As a Gemini family gal, you like to be privy to the minutiae of family members' lives—as bumpy a ride as that can be—because the highs and lows that go with constant communication are preferable to being left out of the so-called loop.

HOW THEY SEE YOU: You're a baffling wonderchild. Only the young and the young at heart understand what you're all about. The others try to wrap their heads around your exploits and adventures, but these experiences are so different from their own that you may as well come from another dimension. With a toss of the hand, they'll comment, "Oh, you're always up to something!"

HOW YOU WANT THEM TO SEE YOU: You wish they'd be impressed! But not in a superficial way—you wish they could acknowledge the things you put your energy into, and validate your choices. If they understood you better, they would. But you should know that they really think you're cool. They just don't understand the kind of effort it takes to accomplish what you have, the way you have.

WHAT THEY LOVE ABOUT YOU (whether they tell you or not): your levity. You personify a breath of fresh air. You know when you're driving down the freeway and you roll the window down and put your hand outside and the rush of air lifts your fingers and your arm can surf on the force of your speed while the wind licks at your flowing hair? Well, you're like that kind of fresh air.

WHAT DRIVES YOU NUTS ABOUT THEM: They can be clueless. Not as individuals, but as a group. That's okay. You're clue-full. Drop those clues, generously and often. Eventually everyone will get the answer, even if you have to supply it for them.

HOLIDAY COPING STRATEGY: Like you need one? Others may get stressed over the hubbub of the holidays, but not you. You revel in the hilarious fragments of conversation, the lively exchanges of advice, gifts, food, and wit—I mean, what is there to stress over? "Live and let live" is your attitude—it serves you well in formal or informal situations, and applies whether there are three or three hundred individuals to "let live."

STELLAR FAMILY ACTIVITIES: parties, games (especially car games), word games, trivia games, activities that involve pets (like training them, caring for them, walking them, and playing with them), dinner table conversations.

Gemini mothers are: **clever**
Gemini daughters are: **witty**
Gemini sisters are: **fun**
Gemini wives are: **spirited**

★ CANCER ★

COMMUNICATING: You don't have to touch base often to touch base well. For you it's more about the intimacy of sharing deeply rooted feelings than the frequency. So you can go weeks, even months, without talking to a relative, and then when you do connect, it's like no time has elapsed. And though you can be guarded with the rest of the world, your next of kin can crack your defenses like a silver crab hammer. Thus, they can easily wound you or set your heart on a glee ride in a single gesture.

HOW THEY SEE YOU: You're home personified—familiarity, complexity, and comfort. They feel they can be themselves around you, without airs, without trying too hard—or sometimes without trying hard enough. You get both the unvarnished version of your family and the unkempt version.

HOW YOU WANT THEM TO SEE YOU: exactly as they do. You believe that everyone has a right to their experience of you, and you're not about to work hard at making them have any particular opinion.

WHAT THEY LOVE ABOUT YOU (whether they tell you or not): your unconditional acceptance. You really strive to embrace your people and their circumstances exactly as they are. And you often get the same inclusive response from them.

WHAT DRIVES YOU NUTS ABOUT THEM: They're so comfortable around you that they have no problem showing up unannounced, venting their issues on your answering machine, or generally blurring the line between the two types of problems in the world: "my problem" and "your problem."

HOLIDAY COPING STRATEGY: There's no getting around it, so you may as well own it: Much of the cooking, entertaining, lodging, gifting, and generally managing falls on your shoulders. This happens every year. In fact, even when you try to ignore the holidays, they wind up happening to you. Taking on responsibility for the holidays is like a compulsion—you can't *not* do it. So get lots of sleep. Otherwise, you're irritable. Also, do what the malls and stores do: Start your holiday plans a little earlier each year.

STELLAR FAMILY ACTIVITIES: cooking, building things, home improvement, hanging out together and doing nothing, talking about other families, playing instruments, listening to music.

Cancer mothers are: **soulful**
Cancer daughters are: **conscientious**
Cancer sisters are: **smart**
Cancer wives are: **perceptive**

★ **LEO** ★

COMMUNICATING: It's not what you say, it's how you say it that makes you a favorite in your family. You turn ordinary daily interactions into a kind of personal theater—amusing, vivid, and memorable—that requires almost no effort on your part. You have sensitized yourself to see the novelty in a situation, and so it pops out at you and you play with it—that's just who you are. So, while others may earn familial attention and adoration through being thoughtful, hardworking, or helpful, you get what you need by just being you.

HOW THEY SEE YOU: You're the fun one. Part mega-talent, part clown. Which part is which is anyone's guess.

HOW YOU WANT THEM TO SEE YOU: You don't really care, as long as it keeps them smiling, laughing, talking about you, and, of course, applauding.

WHAT THEY LOVE ABOUT YOU (whether they tell you or not): your ability to make them feel special. In addition to being your people, they are characters in your story. You study them with the affection of a playwright studying the subjects of her next masterpiece.

★ SHE'S A LEO ★

Though Pisces is the sign often associated with music, dance, and drama, it's Leo who's always been the true entertainer of the zodiac, less concerned with *how* she delights (shocks, mind-blows), just as long as she does. So I ask you: What other sign could MADONNA be? In every evolution of her persona, this lioness has kept us riveted. She caused a sensation with a seemingly innocent song, "Like a Virgin," and has made headlines with taboo images, incendiary relationships, and spiritual awakenings. And now it's motherhood that Madonna's humanitarian efforts are thrusting into the sunshine of hyperconsciousness. So never let it be said that the attention-hogging quality native to Leo's personality is selfish. After all, like Madonna, most Leo women learn to use their astral superpowers for good.

WHAT DRIVES YOU NUTS ABOUT THEM: You wish you could do more for them. Everyone is so gracious and giving toward you that at times you feel you can never catch up, and the truth is, you never will. When you're thoughtful, they're even more thoughtful. So what you need to learn to do is be an expert at receiving. Because a beautifully executed, enthusiastic reception can be a gift in itself.

HOLIDAY COPING STRATEGY: It seems terribly out of character, but you can be a real holiday scrooge. Why? Not because you don't want to celebrate, but because the pressure you feel to perform can be overwhelming. And, to make matters worse, you feel that you must put your personal style stamp on every gift, gesture, and sentiment you extend to your peeps. Store-bought cards just don't say everything you have in your heart! So the following advice will either liberate you or infuriate you, but here it goes: Conform! Buy the store cards and sign them—you're done. If you simply cannot force yourself to conform, then my follow-up advice is to go easy on yourself, especially if you have a big family.

STELLAR FAMILY ACTIVITIES: seeing theater and putting it on together, watching awards shows, partaking in Hollywood gossip, playing with children (especially the ten-and-under set), crocheting, doing paper crafts, decorating for parties.

Leo mothers are: **sunny**

Leo daughters are: **heartwarming**

Leo sisters are: **protective**

Leo wives are: **generous**

★ VIRGO ★

COMMUNICATING: Words, shmerds. A well-prepared dinner can say, "I love you." A ride to the store can say, "You matter to me." And showing up for the recital, promotion, or softball game says, "I'm there for you." This is how you prefer to embrace your loved ones—by honoring them with real action. When there are problems, you solve them by employing the opposite tactic—doing nothing—in hopes that the issue will go away. It's amazing how brilliantly this works out. Why get riled up and exert energy fighting? Ignore, ignore, ignore. In time all relationship kinks work out on their own.

HOW THEY SEE YOU: You're an inspiration for improvement. Your opinions may not be easy to hear sometimes, but they know that you call it as you see it. You feel you would be doing your loved ones a disservice by flattering them when the straight truth will help them grow.

HOW YOU WANT THEM TO SEE YOU: as someone who is on their side.

WHAT THEY LOVE ABOUT YOU (whether they tell you or not): your ordered approach to life. (I feel you rolling your eyes, Virgo. *Yes, Holiday, so I'm obsessive. Don't you have anything more glamorous to give me?* Oh, dear Virgo. If you only knew how adorable and comforting your neurotic habits are. They make the rest of us relax because we know you've done all the checking, worrying, and arranging for us. Thanks for that, btw.)

WHAT DRIVES YOU NUTS ABOUT THEM: They expect you to do all the checking, worrying, and arranging for you. Yeesh.

HOLIDAY COPING STRATEGY: Take that extra-long list you made of must-do holiday preparations—everything from wrapping presents to picking up Aunt Jan at the airport—and rip it in half. There; that's how much you can comfortably do and still have fun. Kindly hand the other half to your mother, sister, assistant, significant other, or person holding a WILL WORK FOR FOOD sign at the bottom of the freeway exit. Wish them good luck and hope for the best.

STELLAR FAMILY ACTIVITIES: gardening, hiking, picnics, festivals, celebrating family members, outings with the whole gang, learning activities, exercise.

Virgo mothers are: **nurturing**

Virgo daughters are: **genuine**

Virgo sisters are: **insightful**

Virgo wives are: **inspiring**

★ LIBRA ★

COMMUNICATING: Your roles as peacekeeper, diplomat, and ambassador are so crucial to your family's health that I pity the Libra-less families. (You know, them. They're the ones who wind up on the evening news because nobody talked crazy Uncle Ned out of racing a truck through the back yard and into the living room.) This brings me to an existential question: If a tree falls (or gets driven into) in your family's back yard, and nobody argues over whose fault it was, are you still needed? *Of course.* In sickness and in health, crisis and boredom, litigation and resolution through third-party arbitration, your easygoing expression and rare listening skills have an integral place in your family dynamic.

HOW THEY SEE YOU: as being on their side. All of them see you this way. How can you be on everyone's side at once? I don't know! But you are. You're really amazing.

HOW YOU WANT THEM TO SEE YOU: as more than their problem-solver.

★ ASTROLOGICAL QUESTION ★

"I am a Libra mom with a Gemini daughter. Often when she's at school, I feel as though I am being summoned by her. But when I pick her up, she says everything was fine. What's going on?"

Separation anxiety a is normal part of Libran living. The closeness you feel with your Gemini daughter is made even more intense by the intellectual similarities and communication style you share—you are two air signs who can communicate like children holding Styrofoam cups connected by string. When there is distance between the cups, the string is still able to carry a message. Even when you're distant from your Gemini, you are tuning in to her thoughts. And though she is happy at school, she, like every other child, probably experiences moments of intensity—moments that are charged with the electricity of interest, joy, anxiety, discovery, pride, and so on. Those are the moments she subconsciously "summons" you, as you likely provide subliminal guidance and security.

Try responding on a conscious level. Send affirming messages mentally to your Gemini, assuring her that she is smart, safe, and so loved. This empowering gesture will also serve to quell your separation anxiety.

In fact, you periodically create a few problems for everyone else to solve, just to even the score.

WHAT THEY LOVE ABOUT YOU (whether they tell you or not): your beauty, aesthetic sense, and ability to turn a humdrum dinner table into a magazine-worthy spread.

WHAT DRIVES YOU NUTS ABOUT THEM: They're crazy, aren't they? You often feel like that normal daughter in the Addams family. But c'mon, admit it. You're glad for their kooky, monstrous qualities because they make you look so sympathetically sane in comparison.

HOLIDAY COPING STRATEGY: Give up trying to make sure everyone is taken care of, and revel in the part of the holiday that makes your heart soar. Officially, that's the religious part, right? You're so correct. But unofficially, it's all about the decorating. So get out your snowblower, glitter glue, and cake-decorating tips and holiday-ize to your heart's content. Your family will thank you for it and be much happier than they would have been had you concentrated on making sure they all got along and were given equal numbers of presents to open.

STELLAR FAMILY ACTIVITIES: going to the zoo, skating, tennis, seeing art, visiting museums, horseback excursions and competitions, drawing up paperwork for life's various passages.

Libra mothers are: **adoring**

Libra daughters are: **felicitous**

Libra sisters are: **stylish**

Libra wives are: **savvy**

★ SCORPIO ★

COMMUNICATING: You're willing to think the best of your people, as long as the "best" comes at a fair market value. In other words, let's be real: There are no bad guys or good guys; there are just people who are born into or embraced by a certain circle, doing their darnedest to make it all work. When it comes to listening to and interacting with the goings-on of your clan, you do these things with a sort of psychic x-ray vision. (Sure, face value is the value you prefer, but alas, you know better.) As far as family is concerned, the three-foot circumference around you might as well be named the "no-spin zone," because you're having none of the bullshit.

HOW THEY SEE YOU: as a tearjerker. Because the truth will do that, and you're in love with the truth. Whether they cry when you're walking down the aisle, or when you're relaying a touching family story, or when you're giving a sincere and overdue compliment, you go straight to the tear ducts, twist, and release. Aww!

HOW YOU WANT THEM TO SEE YOU: Oh, please. When was the last time you cared how anyone saw you?

WHAT THEY LOVE ABOUT YOU (whether they tell you or not): that you're cool. Cousins, new babies, great-grandparents, and aunts . . . you relate to all generations of your people in the same manner. You're respectful, but you don't base your responses on an age bias.

WHAT DRIVES YOU NUTS ABOUT THEM: everything and nothing, depending on your mood. Say your mom tells a not-so-flattering story about you in front of your new beau. On a good day, that's no big deal. But on a bad day, that's cause for a restraining order against her. Oh, you! So extreme.

HOLIDAY COPING STRATEGY: Remember that the most important criterion for determining the success or failure of any family gathering is how well you connect with others. Nothing else really matters. So as long as you're bringing your most sincere self to the party, it will be a win. Because for all your resistance to the hoopla, deep down you only want to love and be loved. And that's what these special days are all about. (Obviously, they're also about who gets what from whom and how much it costs, but who's keeping track?)

STELLAR FAMILY ACTIVITIES: games like Truth or Dare, motocross, cycling, bungee jumping, scuba diving, visiting an array of different kinds of psychics, keeping family secrets, creating mysteries for others to solve.

Scorpio mothers are: **astute**
Scorpio daughters are: **rebellious**
Scorpio sisters are: **enlightening**
Scorpio wives are: **mysterious**

★ SAGITTARIUS ★

COMMUNICATING: Sagittarius, Sagittarius, quite contrary-ous, how does your family tree grow? With babies and marriages, some hilarious, and new ideas right in a row. And whether or not you get married and have children, the new-ideas category is in your realm of responsibility. If you're not introducing at least three new ideas a month to your family, you're not pulling your weight. I'm not talking about discoveries in quantum physics here. I'm talking, "Look, Mom—I put peas in the macaroni!" Or, "Hey, bro, you should try that pizza joint on the corner." And occasionally, you will have the idea that changes your whole family. Like, "Sis, I'd like you to meet Bob," or, "Let's set up video conferencing so we can talk to the grandparents in Alaska face-to-face!"

HOW THEY SEE YOU: as their lucky charm. You are, you know.

HOW YOU WANT THEM TO SEE YOU: as the first person they call when fun opportunities come up. Trip to Vegas? You have your bag packed already. Need a house-sitter for your beach house? What a coinkydink! I just bought a bikini.

WHAT THEY LOVE ABOUT YOU (whether they tell you or not): your spontaneity. It seems that no matter what the adventure is, you're good to go.

WHAT DRIVES YOU NUTS ABOUT THEM: They take everything so seriously. Come on, family—life is for the living, so get out your Amex cards and rack up some frequent flier miles! Oh yeah, and Dad, can I borrow a couple hundred bucks for souvies?

HOLIDAY COPING STRATEGY: Ah, the holidays. All the diverse personalities of your family coming together in the name of goodwill and togetherness. Every year is different. You just don't know what's going to happen, but it can't be good. Or rather, it can't be better than that exotic trip to a remote part of Mexico you've been planning for months. Well, sometimes you actually do stay home for the holidays, but you like to spend at least every other year doing your thing, your way.

STELLAR FAMILY ACTIVITIES: tours, garage sales, art fairs, fairs and festivals of any kind, camping, jet-setting, concert-going, trains, planes, and automobile trips.

Sagittarius mothers are: **motivational**
Sagittarius daughters are: **spunky**
Sagittarius sisters are: **sassy**
Sagittarius wives are: **vivacious**

★CAPRICORN★

COMMUNICATING: You are the keeper of family tradition, the master of ceremonies for sacred family rituals. And by sacred family rituals, I'm not talking candles in a circle and chanting in special robes. I'm talking everyone showing up for Sunday dinner, and no cell phones at the table, for Pete's sake! It's the habits you establish as a group that make you strong—and someone has to make sure they are honored properly. If it weren't for you, these important moments of togetherness might be taken too lightly, or forgotten.

HOW THEY SEE YOU: as the Godfather . . . er, Godmother. You may as well be talking like you have cotton stuffed in your cheeks, for all the reverence your family has for you. It's well deserved, of course. (And I'm not just saying that because I'm afraid of waking up with a severed horse's head as a bedfellow.)

HOW YOU WANT THEM TO SEE YOU: as a nice girl. A good girl. A girl who loves them and does her best to show it, mostly by being sweet and understanding, and sometimes by being harsh.

WHAT THEY LOVE ABOUT YOU (whether they tell you or not): your powerful presence—they feel safe around you. And the care and priority you give to your family unit make them proud to be a part of it.

WHAT DRIVES YOU NUTS ABOUT THEM: They don't have the same priorities as you, and sometimes they even have the nerve to point this out, as if their priorities were more correct. If they would just snap to the world according to you, things would be much easier. But *noooooo. . . .*

HOLIDAY COPING STRATEGY: I would tell you to adopt the California-surfer-girl attitude of "It's all good," but you and I both know that's too much of a stretch. It's not all good, especially around the holidays. Sometimes the people you want to be there aren't there, and the ones you don't want to be there are present in full force. You get gifts for people who didn't get one for you, and people give you gifts whom you don't have gifts for. There are never enough chairs or matching silverware. You inevitably run out of something important, like eggs, toilet paper, or antidepressants. So for me to tell you, "It's all good," well, that would just be rude. Instead I'd like to gently suggest that it's not all bad. And, in fact, the things that might be considered bad might give personality to your family time together, and give you a story for later.

STELLAR FAMILY ACTIVITIES: attending services, reciting, remembering, performing, cleaning, budgeting, shopping, discussing politics, baking.

Capricorn mothers are: **humorists**
Capricorn daughters are: **problem-solvers**
Capricorn sisters are: **advisors**
Capricorn wives are: **queens**

★AQUARIUS★

COMMUNICATING: The easy popularity you enjoy with friends extends into your family circle—or perhaps it's the other way around. Either way, you're well liked for a reason. Your motto is to accept others as they are and help where you can. To the untrained observer, the services you provide for your family members might be seen as generous, charitable, or even saintly. What they don't know is that you're actually an opportunist. It just so happens that when you're kind and laid-back, your family feels inclined to give you sweet perks—the keys to the good car, dibs on a family heirloom, a surprise check to help you out with a project. . . . It's like once you start the cycle of giving, your life becomes a never-ending spiral of thank-you notes!

HOW THEY SEE YOU: as the future of their dreams. You pave the way for whatever they haven't figured out how to make real in their lives. Your innovation and belief in tomorrow inspire them to move forward.

HOW YOU WANT THEM TO SEE YOU: as clever and able. You may accept the help that is given to you, but that doesn't mean you couldn't have done it on your own. You want to know that they know that.

WHAT THEY LOVE ABOUT YOU (whether they tell you or not): your wacky ideas. Especially the ones that don't even make sense. Girl, sometimes it's like you speak a different language from the rest of your clan with your surrealist fantasy talk. It's a good thing that one doesn't need to understand you in order to appreciate you.

WHAT DRIVES YOU NUTS ABOUT THEM: They can be so stiff! So correct! So boring! You make it your personal mission to shock the bourgeoisie in the manner of a daring French dadaist. Doing so might involve a whoopee cushion, streaking, or coming to dinner in a top hat made of raisin toast.

HOLIDAY COPING STRATEGY: Setting differences aside is your usual habit. During the holidays it helps to broaden that rule to include not only differences, but expectations, judgments, grievances, and your attachment to any outcome whatsoever. This is hard. But if you can let go of this sort of family baggage, you achieve a personal Zen state of family unity that everyone in your family can feel, whether they ascribe to that state or not. The Zen state of family unity may be fleeting, but keep believing you can return there—this is how world peace begins.

STELLAR FAMILY ACTIVITIES: games, brainteasers, fundraising, discussing philosophy, dancing, daydreaming, planning for the future, celebrating one another's uniqueness.

Aquarius mothers are: **lighthearted**
Aquarius daughters are: **magical**
Aquarius sisters are: **enthusiastic**
Aquarius wives are: **whimsical**

 ★ PISCES ★

COMMUNICATING: You know how when you were a kid, you traveled to see distant relatives every year or so and they would comment endlessly about how you'd grown, and how they hardly recognized you? Well, as a Pisces you never quite grow out of that phase. No matter how old you are, it's like family has to readjust to a new you every time they see you. You're constantly evolving as a person—it's part of the way you interact with the world, letting it influence you in different ways every day. Anyway, there's this awkward getting-reacquainted thing you do with family with each encounter. The nice part is that family really does want to get up to speed and is always excited to learn who you are this time.

HOW THEY SEE YOU: You're the spiritual touchstone of the group. They relate to you on many levels at once, and feel a strong connection. Often they'll let you know things that no one else in the family is privy to.

HOW YOU WANT THEM TO SEE YOU: as someone they can come to if they need to, but not as someone they must call compulsively and vent to every time something goes wrong for them. You're compassionate, but you also have a life, people!

WHAT THEY LOVE ABOUT YOU (whether they tell you or not): your wisdom. And it doesn't mean that you know the perfect thing to say, or can supply the solution. But you know how to be present and connect in a healing way as only the truly wise can.

WHAT DRIVES YOU NUTS ABOUT THEM: not much, really. You think their quirks are cute and their faults make them human. Still, as much as you like being around them, there are times when you feel as though you'll lose your mind if you don't get away from them, and fast.

HOLIDAY COPING STRATEGY: Your creativity is key to keeping the holidays bright. Because a creative Pisces is a happy Pisces. And a Pisces who isn't indulging her proclivities and exploring her talents is cranky when there are too many people vying for quality time and attention. Projects that tickle different parts of your brain, and give your heart expression and your intuition a channel to work through, will keep your mood light while you produce wonderful gifts and decorations that will ultimately be keepsakes to remind you later about the special times you spent with your clan.

STELLAR FAMILY ACTIVITIES: spiritual studies, listening to and playing music, swimming, water sports, beach time, prayer, long walks in nature together.

Pisces mothers are: **mystics**
Pisces daughters are: **muses**
Pisces sisters are: **precocious**
Pisces wives are: **mesmerizing**

om at home

HOME DESIGN

I am not my environment. I am not my environment. I am not my environment. I repeat this mantra to myself after receiving a mighty disturbing phone call from my husband. He is ten minutes away, he says. He is bringing a band with him. *A band.* How many people is that? I ask. It's five. Oh yeah, and a sound guy. So that's six. Don't worry, they just want to hang out and watch a fight on HBO. Can I call up and order it on Pay-Per-View? I hang up and look around at a sink full of dirty dishes, a floor scattered with laundry, and a counter stacked high with a landslide of papers. Yes, I decide, I can order a fight. Just perhaps not the fight he was expecting.

I am not my environment. The mantra starts, and so does my wondering. If I am not my environment, then why do I feel so ashamed at the prospect of surprise visitors catching me with my domestic pants down?

The answer comes to me as such: Environments matter. They are the external expression of an internal being. And when that internal being is exposed as being perhaps a bit unorganized, untidy, unfinished, or—worst of all to a Leo like me, gasp—unstyled . . . well, it's unsettling, to say the least. Leos' homes are our movie sets. When they're not properly erected by the time the audience arrives, the whole show suffers. It's a similar situation for Venus-ruled Libras and Taureans—they're super-aesthetic types who are constantly comparing their environs to the pages of magazines. They cringe when their own digs aren't photograph-ready.

And even if your own personal mess isn't exposed to the rest of the world, because, say—and I'm just being hypothetical here—in ten minutes you are able to remove all dishes, laundry, and clutter from your living room and kitchen and hide them behind the curtain of your bathtub— does that make it better? I mean, is it really right that other people get to enjoy a more pleasing environment than you would allow yourself?

I find that it's the little things that eat away at a girl's psyche—and ultimately her self-esteem. The cluster of pole-like objects that have been in the back of the linen closet for three years—what exactly are they? Only the spiders know. That odd-size lightbulb in the antique bedroom lamp that burned out sometime during the rockabilly fad—where am I supposed to buy more of those? The broken printer under the office desk. The tangle of apparently essential cords in the bottom drawer—wait, which goes to what? The pile of magazines, the picture you've been meaning to frame, the fame you've been meaning to nail to the wall.

Kind of hard to feel inner peace when you're living in outer *ugh*.

Here is an illustration that describes how a pile of papers can eat away at a girl's fragile sense of self:

The eyes see a pile of papers. Thought: *That's a pile of paper. I should file those. I need to file those. But I don't have time now, I have so much to do—I have to go the post office before it closes, send a birthday present to my niece, take the car in for an oil change, drop that pile of shirts off at the dry cleaners, watch* Oprah. *It's all so overwhelming! If only I were the kind of person who could handle it all. But I can't! I can't handle my home, I can't handle my life! I'm completely falling apart! Oh, and I'm hungry, too.*

I'm convinced that guys do not have the same experience. This, I am sure, is the male version of the same thought pattern:

The eyes see a pile of papers. Thought: *That's a pile of paper. I'm hungry.*

I do have girlfriends whom I can sneak up on at home, any time of day, any day of the week, and their houses look like they were just in professional photo shoots for Pottery Barn, *Yogi Times,* or *Better Homes and Gardens,* depending on the girlfriend. Boy, do those girls annoy me. Most of them are Virgos or have Virgo rising—oh-so-orderly girls who get a druglike rush from organizing CD collections and perfectly aligning the spoons in their silverware drawers.

I, Holiday Mathis, must confess that I have neither the stars, nor the genes, nor the skill set, nor the innate desire, to achieve domestic perfection.

What I do have, however, is the astrological edge. And that's all I need to make my less-than-perfect domestic scene not only work for me, but be something I can ultimately be proud of when someone, or *a whole band* (plus a sound guy), pops in to watch a fight. (Preferably on TV.)

Like today. I hear a car roll up the driveway, and I look around at my house. Yes, I've done some kamikaze sweeping under the carpet (or into the bathtub, as the case may be). But most of the congregations of clutter I leave where they are, and instead I focus on the whole picture: at the brightly colored kitchen, done up in social, cheery Sagittarian hues of turquoise and an electric yellow-green—it's a happy, upbeat room, one that's not overly appetite-stimulating (to help us quit eating while we're ahead). This area has been the center of many a boisterous conversation—we chose these Sagittarian colors because they catalyze a surge of energy, encouraging opinion and awareness.

Now it's your turn. Look around your pad. You thought you had problems that only a gaggle of queer eyes could fix, but maybe there's another way to handle what ails you, and to help you find our own *om* at home:

- **Do you have trouble concentrating while sitting at your home desk?** Pull in some Taurus energy and get to work. Taurus energy is steadfast and methodical. It's not easily distracted and it plods on, step by step, until the task is done. Plus, it attracts money.
- **Are you doing the diet thing?** Bring high-strung Aries or energetic Sagittarian vibes into the kitchen. These are calorie-burning fire-sign vibes that keep your metabolism up.
- **No cell service? Is your Internet hookup a letdown?** Get Gemini on the job for fast, effortless communication. Gemini energy is the master of easy connections and information flow.

Maybe we are not our environments. But, as with our environments, there's a little bit of every sign in all of us. All we have to do is touch on it to solve the problem at hand.

Here's a chance for a gal to call on her planetary sisters to customize the perfect home environment for her lifestyle goals. Read on to find out where and how to astral–feng shui your way into the ideal pad.

★ ARIES ★

If you are an Aries, your home is your crash pad. In fact, it may take you until your thirties or forties to finally decide to go all out and personalize your decor. You especially resonate with bright colors and busy, vibrant patterns. Consider pulling heavily on the energies of Cancer and Libra to create balance in your abode.

ANY SIGN CAN INVOKE THE ENERGY OF ARIES. Where should you? In an exercise room or area, in a high-energy kitchen where weight control is the aim, and anywhere you go to feel awake and feisty—ready to take on the world. If you are a lawyer, a salesperson, or a comedian, definitely use bits of Aries energy to sharpen your "killer" edge.

KEY ARIES-DECOR WORDS: Excitement, weight loss, protection. The Ram's warrior spirit is all about protection, vitality, ferocity, shock! These qualities should be used sparingly in your haven, no matter what sign you are. Still, Aries touches add the "pow" that takes home design to the "wow and now" level.

HINT: It's nothing you can buy at Pottery Barn. Aries energy is in your face. When your eyes land on an Aries item, your pupils automatically dilate. It's the hot-red throw pillow on an olive-colored couch. It's the extra-tall lava lamp in the corner. It's the decorative sword mounted above the fireplace mantel that makes people think, *Hmm . . . shy Suzy has another side to her, doesn't she?*

TIP: Live in a rough hood? Adorn your front door with the protective energy of Aries. Paint it red or gold. Add a door knocker in red or gold.

ASTRAL ALERT: Avoid bringing Aries energy into your bedroom. It's not very restful, and if you're part of a couple, it can cause fighting.

Aries colors: **red, black, and gold**
Aries metal: **iron**
Aries flowers: **tiger lily, geranium, roses with the thorns still on**

INCREASE YOUR ARIES POWER WITH: candles, a fire in the fireplace, a fire pit outside, brightly colored art, a red wall, incense, dragon imagery, swords and weapons, busts (as in a sculpture of someone's head), taxidermy, animal bones and horns.

ON ARIES' DOMESTIC SOUND TRACK: "Rebel Yell," by Billy Idol; "Mr. Brightside," by The Killers; "We Didn't Start The Fire," by Billy Joel.

★ TAURUS ★

If you are a Taurus, home is where you chill your Veuve Clicquot. It's your opulent palace, even it it's only a studio apartment. It's where you stash your diamonds and lavish in extra-long bubble baths. You hope that visitors will be impressed by a few high-end designer items you've collected over the years. However, every Taurus gal needs to be reminded once in a while that style doesn't have to be costly. You can draw on the energy of Leo and Scorpio to strike a balance between elegance and extravagance.

ANY SIGN CAN INVOKE THE ENERGY OF TAURUS. Where should you? An upwardly mobile gal of any sign must have the Taurus touch in her "money corner." Feng shui methods vary, but contemporary experts define the money corner as the back left corner of a space when you're standing in the doorway facing the space. Also, bring Taurus energy into the place where you pay your bills. Some Taurus energy should hover in the kitchen to inspire delicious cooking, and some belongs in your closet to invoke the goddess of quality.

KEY TAURUS-DECOR WORDS: luxury, designer, wealth. Taurus energy emanates in waves that look suspiciously like dollar signs. In fact, in the cartoon version of Taurus energy, the energy hits the eyeballs, which go all "$$$" to the jingling accompaniment of an opening cash register. In other words, design elements that are Taurean are *phat*. The emphasis is on fine quality, like real leather, handmade craftsmanship, solid hardwood, customization—anything that most people can't afford. Which brings me to the reason one might not Taurus-ize the whole house, unless one happens to have the budget of Paris Hilton.

ASTRAL ALERT: Not too much Taurus energy in the kitchen, my dears, unless your goal is to gain weight.

Taurus colors: **pink, pale blue, green**
Taurus metals: **gold, copper**
Taurus flowers: **orange blossom, freesia, laurel**

INCREASE YOUR TAURUS POWER WITH: sturdy, elegant wood furniture, totally soft textures like cashmere and chenille, anything gilded in real gold, plants—especially small trees, baroque elements, brocade, the scent of citrus, fruit trees growing in the back left corner of a yard.

ON TAURUS'S DOMESTIC SOUND TRACK: "Lucy in the Sky with Diamonds," by The Beatles; "Gold Digger," by Kanye West; "Marriage of Figaro," by Mozart.

★ Gemini ★

If you are a Gemini, your home is your think tank. It's a springboard for your high-energy lifestyle, so it must not only support your physical needs, but continually spark your intellect. So it's ideally a place that attracts people who have ideas, and encourages them to spill 'em when they cross the threshold of your front door. Many a late night will be spent bandying spirited arguments across your kitchen table. Consider drawing on the energy of Virgo and Sagittarius to keep your home in the Zen zone.

ANY SIGN CAN INVOKE THE ENERGY OF GEMINI. Where should you? Your home office, the telephone/fax table, the mailbox. The ideal place for Gemini design elements is anywhere you want to feel conversationally fluent. For instance, if you usually sit in a certain chair when you make your calls, that's where you need a dash of Gemini. The place where you keep your phone, fax, stationery, and mail also benefits from the presence of Gemini energy.

KEY GEMINI-DECOR WORDS: communication, intelligence, fun. Gemini energy sparks conversation. It's that cartoon you cut out and stuck on the refrigerator that causes a chuckle and a follow-up quip from every passerby. It's the group picture in the funky frame that invites visitors to comment, "Looks like a fun crowd. Who are they?" It's the bizarre object on your coffee table that gives you a reason to chat about the art class you took last summer. If it evokes a response, it resonates in the realm of the Twins.

TIP: The best way to bring Gemini energy to your mailbox is to subscribe to periodicals that tickle your intellect. Another way is to have a pen pal— which is such a retro idea, it's new again.

ASTRAL ALERT: Too much Gemini energy in the home office can be hazardous to your production levels unless your business requires that you spend most of your time on the phone. Balance your home office with Virgo energy for organization and Capricorn energy for getting back to the bottom line.

INCREASE YOUR GEMINI POWER WITH: trendy designs, ultra-modern touches, furniture that looks cooler than it is comfortable, rearranging the furniture and the look of a space often, weather thermometers, weather vanes, wind socks, things that spin, such as clocks, any design that incorporates butterflies or dragonflies.

Gemini colors: **light blue, and whatever color is in at the moment**
Gemini metals: **quicksilver, electrum**
Gemini flowers: **magnolia, wisteria, pansy**

ON GEMINI'S DOMESTIC SOUND TRACK: "Fly Away," by Lenny Kravitz; "Don't Stop," by Brazilian Girls; "Chariot," by Gavin DeGraw.

★ CANCER ★

If you are a Cancer, home is your world. You wish you could enclose it—seal it off like an ecodome that is impervious to the weather and goings-on of the outside so-called world. (All the things that really matter happen within your walls, anyway.) Of course, your loved ones would all be invited into the ecodome, too. And perhaps even some strangers who happened to be passing by when the ecodome was open. Because, let's face it, everyone feels comfortable at your place, so you attract many unexpected visitors, from stray cats to stray people. Consider pulling heavily from Libra and Capricorn energies to keep your ecodome perfectly balanced.

ANY SIGN CAN INVOKE THE ENERGY OF CANCER. Where should you? The ideal place for Cancer energy is in the entryway—that first-impression place where you fling open the door and say, "Ahhhhhh" after a long day of work. Cancer energy should also be present in the areas where you're just kickin' it with your nearest and dearest, like the den or the living room.

KEY CANCER-DECOR WORDS: comfort, soothing, connection. Cancer is the mothering energy that home is all about. One might say it's womb-esque.

Cancer energy is represented in the comfort elements that encourage you to be who you are, flaws, talents, and all. Cancer energy is in family photos. It's in the hot tea you serve to someone who has just taken an eight-hour plane ride to see you. Cancer energy is in the soft down cushion you plop down on when you're reading your favorite magazine. Cancer energy is a hug. It's anything that makes you grateful you are finally home sweet home.

ASTRAL ALERT: You know the old adage about fish and visitors—three days is the limit. If you keep getting guests who don't want to leave, you might want to cut back on the Cancer influences in your design.

Cancer colors: **creamy colors that can be found in sea foam, beachy beiges, sandy brown, and silver**

Cancer metal: **silver**

Cancer flowers: **chrysanthemum, larkspur, tuberose**

INCREASE YOUR CANCER POWER WITH: Pearl and mother-of-pearl on furniture or accents, moon images, baking (especially muffins or pie), cooking with rosemary, soft pillows, down, comforters, herbal tea, chicken soup, soft linens.

ON CANCER'S DOMESTIC SOUND TRACK: "Stickwitu," by The Pussycat Dolls; "Moon River" (Stuart Mathis version); "Weather with You," by Crowded House.

★ LEO ★

If you are a Leo, home is your movie set. Your taste tends to be on the grand side because not only are you decorating for yourself, but you also want to make a statement to teach your audience who you are. Bring in the energy of Scorpio and Aquarius to balance your high-intensity environment.

ANY SIGN CAN INVOKE THE ENERGY OF LEO. Where should you? The ideal place to invoke the energy of Leo is where you enjoy your media. Leo energy entices you to go for a ride, so maximize the escapist potential housed inside your entertainment center. It's also fun to bring Leo energy into the place where you get dressed. Leo energy is a not-so-subtle reminder that you are the star in your show, so you'd better give them a reason to man up the follow-spot.

Additionally, if you are lucky enough to have something as majestic as a balcony, I think a touch of Leo, in the form of an eye-catching swing or a potted palm, for instance, makes this area an irresistible feature of your abode.

KEY LEO-DECOR WORDS: drama, playfulness, attention-getting. As the sign of children, Leo energy is dramatic and heightened in a way that could, to the inexperienced, seem childish. But contemporary designers understand that children are living and playing even in households where everyone is over the age of eighteen, because there is a child inside of each of us, stirring with giddy excitement, eager to spring at the slightest provocation. Leo energy calls out, *Ready or not, here I come. . . .* Leo energy is bold colors and big-headed dolls, it's scrolling lines that make a piece of furniture seem fit for a princess, it's the balloon-figure art of Jeff Koons, it's a Post-it note on your mirror that says, "PLAY!"

ASTRAL ALERT: Leo energy is best in small doses—a little makes a big statement.

Leo colors: **gold, orange, yellow**
Leo metal: **gold**
Leo flowers: **sunflower, allium, marigold**

INCREASE YOUR LEO POWER WITH: Mirrors! Outsider art, sun imagery, pictures of iconic film stars, red carpet, Hollywood imagery, especially in the golden era or having to do with the Hollywood sign, palm trees, cameras, bright lighting.

ON LEO'S DOMESTIC SOUNDTRACK: "Only You," by Yaz; "Invisible Sun," by The Police; "Satellite," by Dave Matthews Band.

★ 𝕍𝕀ℝ𝔾𝕆 ★

If you are a Virgo, home is your healing place. It's your center for personal improvement. It's the expression of your nurturing spirit. It's where you get organized. Oh, and it's tidy-clean. (At least, the outside world would judge it as so, and yet oddly, it never seems tidy-clean enough to you.) For balance, call on Sagittarius and Pisces energies in your home as well.

ANY SIGN CAN INVOKE THE ENERGY OF VIRGO. Where should you? The ideal place for Virgo energy is anywhere at all—it's just lovely that way. But it's especially needed where there are many items to keep track of, such as papers, socks, or plants. Virgo energy staves off the mean fairies who steal car keys right when you're running out the door, or hide that tax document under a pile of magazines, so you can have back that fifty minutes a week people spend looking for things. Bring Virgo into your garden, too, as it's the sign of the green thumb. Virgo energy provides the kind of structure that living things need in order to grow.

KEY VIRGO-DECOR WORDS: Growth, health, spotlessness. Virgo energy is all about taking care of business. It's about being organized so that you can grow your talents, explore your world, and live your dreams. Virgo energy is an action plan you jot down in a moment of clarity. It's the sparkling interior of a refrigerator filled with fresh green vegetables. It's the label maker and the alphabetical filing system for your important papers. Truly, Virgo energy has a place in any area of your home. It's also an energy that can be called upon in chaotic times to restore your home's haven status.

ASTRAL ALERT: It's tough for most humans to have too much Virgo energy in a house—living beings affect the environment and make a mess that requires daily restoration. However, if you are one of those rare too-clean types who obsess over minor domestic details, toning down the Virgo energy in your house can help you to relax.

Virgo colors: **green**
Virgo metal: **platinum**
Virgo flowers: **lily, narcissus, veronica**

INCREASE YOUR VIRGO POWER WITH: labels, files, systems of all kinds, organizing bins, thriving plants, a window herb garden, handmade accessories, detailed stitching, needlepoint, spare designs, furniture that is a perfect balance of beautiful form and practical function.

ON VIRGO'S DOMESTIC SOUND TRACK: "Mushaboom," by Feist; "Come Clean," by Hilary Duff; "Steady On," by Shawn Colvin.

★ LIBRA ★

If you are a Libra, home is your neutral territory, your Switzerland. It's the conflict-free zone where you ready yourself for world diplomacy. It's also where you keep your art—the lovely objects that take your mind to an ideal version of life. Draw on Capricorn and Aries energies to add even more intrigue to your domain.

ANY SIGN CAN INVOKE THE ENERGY OF LIBRA. Where should you? The ideal place for Libra energy is wherever fights tend to break out—like the kids' room. Libra energy brings sharing, diplomacy, and harmony, abolishing those annoying screams, "Mom, he hit me—I was playing with it first!" Libra energy in the guest room makes for happier visitors. And Libra energy should always be present in the art you choose—it's present in most art anyhow, as it represents the tenets of artistic symmetry, rhythm, color, texture, skill, and intent.

KEY LIBRA-DECOR WORDS: refined, symmetrical, high-minded.

ASTRAL ALERT: There are occasions when you will need to make a case for yourself, perform an intervention or take a stand. These are the times to tone down the Libra energy around you and bring in the warrior energy of Aries.

Libra colors: **lavender and airy blues**

Libra metal: **brass**

Libra flowers: **daisy, Euphorbea fulgens, hydrangea**

INCREASE YOUR LIBRA POWER WITH: things that come in sets of two, equal distribution of furniture throughout the room, a well-planned lighting scheme, art, art, and more art, elephant symbols, square designs, things that must balance to work properly, such as tops, teeter-totters, and obviously scales

ON LIBRA'S DOMESTIC SOUND TRACK: "I'll Stand by You," by The Pretenders; "You're Beautiful," by James Blunt; "Playground Love," by Air.

★ SCORPIO ★

If you are a Scorpio, your home is the ultimate expression of your subconscious. You can look at the way your papers are laid out on your desk, the arrangement of your toiletries, or the imprint of your head on a pillow, and from these details psychically touch where your mind, heart, and soul are in the present slice of time. You are attracted to designs that embody your more intense moods, and you enjoy when your environment elicits a visceral reaction from you and others. For balance, draw from Aquarius and Taurus energies in your home.

ANY SIGN CAN INVOKE THE ENERGY OF SCORPIO. Where should you? The ideal place for Scorpio energy is your sexy bedroom. As the sign that governs passion, its energy invites the satisfaction of your desire. It's also ideal for the bathroom.

KEY SCORPIO-DECOR WORDS: intensity, privacy, passion. Scorpio is the energy of transformation. It's one part catalyst and one part cocoon. It's crimson sheets of satin where anything might happen. It's a shower that is so hot, it's turning you red while it relaxes you. It's the tweezers that shape your eyebrows as you "ouch, ouch, ouch . . . ah, how pretty." Scorpio energy is halfway between the sleep and the dream. It's surrealist literature and underground music. It's pinup girls and controversial images. It's the deep and weird secret you only share only with your diary.

ASTRAL ALERT: Scorpio energy is a private and seductive energy that most people should not use on the facade of their home or around the front door, as it produces the kind of curiosity that brings unexpected visitors.

Scorpio colors: **dark crimson hues, deep purple, blue-black**
Scorpio metal: **steel**
Scorpio flowers: **gerbera, anthurium, Venus flytrap**

INCREASE YOUR SCORPIO POWER WITH: burgundy, maroon, scarlet . . . on the wall, your bedding, or drapes, or as accent colors. Topaz is Scorpio's favorite stone. Keep one in the nightstand. Moroccan and Tahitian influences invite Scorpio to rule the bedroom, as do gothic influences and anything from New Orleans. Scorpio is the sign of secrets, and anything hidden in the bedroom attracts Scorpio energy. This includes a token under the mattress, a locked box under the bed, or a hidden door in the closet. Dim lighting allows Scorpio energy to rule the other senses. Scorpio is more about feeling than seeing, anyway.

ON SCORPIO'S DOMESTIC SOUND TRACK: "I Will Follow You into the Dark," by Death Cab for Cutie; "I Will Survive" (Cake version); "Essence," by Lucinda Williams.

★ＳAGITTARIUS★

If you are a Sagittarius, home is where you sleep—which, btw, is not the same place as where your mail gets sent to you. Home is a state of mind that you carry with you wherever your travels may take you. Home is essentially your ability to make yourself comfortable wherever you are. And as for that place where the mail comes, you can certainly benefit from the balance that Pisces and Gemini energies will bring to it.

★ SHE'S A Sagittarius ★

JANE AUSTEN rocks my bonnet. If that surprises you, think about this: The spirit of rock is not about a drumbeat, a hairstyle, or an electric guitar. It's about living your own personal revolution at stadium-level volume—even if the revolt in question makes about as much noise as, say, a woman sitting at a desk, scribbling with one of those scratchy quill pens. Such was the rebellion of fire sign Jane Austen, who set the publishing world ablaze with her stories of a different kind of womanhood. Austen's women were intelligent, sassy sorts who, if they couldn't marry for love, would rather (gasp!) go the indie way and avoid matrimony altogether. Sagittarius is the sign of the fearless pioneer, and Miss Austen was a firebrand in her own right—bonnet and all.

ANY SIGN CAN INVOKE THE ENERGY OF SAGITTARIUS. Where should you? The ideal place for on-the-go Sagittarius energy is in your car, in your windows, and in your storage areas. The car is obvious, because Sagittarius is not only about going to the cool places, it's also about turning up the tunes and rocking out to the vivid adventure that blurs your windshield along the way. As far as the windows go, it's simple: Sagittarius energy frames the view. In regard to storage, Sagittarius energy encourages you to have very little in the way of things worthy of preserving. The lighter your baggage, the freer you'll feel on life's adventure.

KEY SAGITTARIUS-DECOR WORDS: adventure, worldview, optimism. Sagittarius energy is an arrow aimed at Jupiter that lands in a yard on the other side of the world, and you're compelled to retrieve it. It's a book of photography that makes you long to know Egypt. It's a Chinese coin on the windowsill that reminds you that there are countless currencies and values in the world to choose from. It's the unusual charm you hang from the rearview mirror to psychically deflect the radar speed gun and attract fabulous parking spaces.

ASTRAL ALERT: The high buzz of Sagittarius energy is the opposite of comforting; it's more like a kick in the pants. This is not an energy to draw into areas where you go to relax.

Sagittarius colors: **turquoise and electric colors like lime and tangerine**

Sagittarius metal: **bronze**

Sagittarius flowers: **tulip, bird-of-paradise, protea**

INCREASE YOUR SAGITTARIUS POWER WITH: globes, collages, influences from any culture foreign to your own, telescopes, binoculars, books and DVDs in other languages, maps, compasses, GPS devices.

ON SAGITTARIUS'S DOMESTIC SOUND TRACK: "Like a Rolling Stone," by Bob Dylan; "I Melt with You," by Modern English; "So Many Nites," by Manu Chao.

★ CAPRICORN ★

If you are a Capricorn, home is your Fortune 500 company, of which you, of course, are the CEO. The product? The best you that you can be. Home is where you are respected and honored, and where you pay homage to those whom you respect and honor. Home is where you feel most industrious, and where the fruits of your labor are appreciated. You balance your home well when you also pull from the energies of Aries and Cancer.

ANY SIGN CAN INVOKE THE ENERGY OF CAPRICORN. Where should you? Wherever you'd like to evoke the traditional, especially in a dining room table or mantelpiece. Also call Capricorn into your wardrobe, because every woman should have some version of the ultimate Capricorn talisman—a power suit. The bathroom mirror is also a Capricorn zone when you dare to adorn it with messages designed to send you on your upwardly mobile way.

KEY CAPRICORN-DECOR WORDS: power, tradition, rulership. Capricorn energy has the look and feel of importance. It says, *I'm here, and I'm not going anywhere, so live with me.* It's the heirloom furniture where you keep the pictures of your ancestors. It's the hardwood dining room table that will be a memory-teaser for future generations. It's the mantel where you light candles and make meaningful announcements, or honor significant days. Capricorn energy is a wax seal on your letters or the classic pattern of your china. It's the formalities of your domestic life.

ASTRAL ALERT: Too much Capricorn energy can be stodgy if not tempered by modern influences. Mix the old with the new, and you can't go wrong.

Capricorn colors: **gray, navy, burgundy, teal**

Capricorn metal: **tin**

Capricorn flowers: **gardenia, poinsettia, Queen Anne's lace**

INCREASE YOUR CAPRICORN POWER WITH: antiques, heirlooms, family trees, family crests, ornate symbols such as Fabergé eggs, chandeliers, reference books and books of higher learning, aged leather, awards of any kind, especially plaques and trophies.

ON CAPRICORN'S DOMESTIC SOUND TRACK: "Ain't No Mountain High Enough," by Marvin Gaye and Tammi Terrell; "Solitude Standing," by Suzanne Vega; "Wildflowers" ("You Belong"), by Tom Petty.

★AQUARIUS★

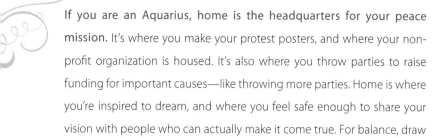

If you are an Aquarius, home is the headquarters for your peace mission. It's where you make your protest posters, and where your nonprofit organization is housed. It's also where you throw parties to raise funding for important causes—like throwing more parties. Home is where you're inspired to dream, and where you feel safe enough to share your vision with people who can actually make it come true. For balance, draw on the energies of Taurus and Leo.

ANY SIGN CAN INVOKE THE ENERGY OF AQUARIUS. Where should you? You definitely need the high-tech juju of Aquarius around your more complicated household equipment, such as television recording devices, iPods, alarm systems, watering systems, and lighting and sound systems. Aquarius is about figuring it out fast and using it easily. The laundry and utility areas of your home can also use the good-luck energy of the water bearer.

KEY AQUARIUS-DECOR WORDS: helping, advancement, future. Aquarius is the sign of tomorrow. It's attracted to progress, especially the kind that helps people do things faster, better, and easier. Aquarius energy is present in the automatic-drip coffee machine that wakes up before you do. It's in the super-quick Internet connection that allows you to do your grocery shopping online. But it's not just in things that can be plugged into your wall. Aquarius energy is present wherever there are people helping people. Anything that reminds you to give of yourself—a ticket to a charity event, a flyer about the present need of others in your community, or a donation box that's a fixture of your pantry or closet—is teeming with Aquarius energy.

ASTRAL ALERT: Remember that you have to take care of yourself first to be able to give to others. When you feel tapped out, tone down the Aquarius energy and draw on Pisces or Leo.

Aquarius colors: **violet; neons; shimmering, opalescent pinks and blues**

Aquarius metal: **lead**

Aquarius flowers: **orchid, primrose, heather**

INCREASE YOUR AQUARIUS POWER WITH: specialized cases and organizers for electronic equipment, fans that keep computers at lower temperatures, sparkly personalization on equipment like iPods and cell phones, accessories for your equipment, peacock feathers, vases and urns, small windup toys or robots.

ON AQUARIUS'S DOMESTIC SOUND TRACK: "Put Your Records On," by Corinne Bailey Rae; "What the World Needs Now," by Dionne Warwick; "Imagine," by John Lennon.

★ PISCES ★

If you are a Pisces, home is your yoga studio, your reflection pool, your **dreamscape.** It's where you return to center and recharge your creativity. It's the expression of your soul's journey. The one thing you require more than any other design element in your Pisces home is space. For you, clutter and restriction are the antitheses of comfort. Your ideal abode is somewhere where your mind can soar to ethereal places without getting bogged down by such mundane details as piles of bills and laundry. For balance, bring Gemini and Virgo energies into your home.

ANY SIGN CAN INVOKE THE ENERGY OF PISCES. Where should you? Definitely in the places where you meditate, listen to music, stretch, daydream, write down your dreams, and generally chill out.

KEY PISCES-DECOR WORDS: spirit, holistic, *ommmmmm*. Pisces energy in design relies on sacred geometry. It's natural and simple, yet it evokes a mystical feeling. If you have ever followed the logarithmic spirals of a chambered nautilus shell with your eyes, you've been inside the magical simplicity of Piscean energy. It's in the minuscule ripples of water your goldfish creates with his mouth when he eats a piece of floating food. It's in the small ribbon of smoke streaming from a lit stick of incense. It's in your dream journal, where you structure the infinite possibilities of your creative subconscious.

ASTRAL ALERT: Pisces energy is fabulous for starting a conversation with your own higher self, but it's not so great for starting conversations with other people. So if you're having friends over, bring in Gemini energy to disturb the peace in your Pisces zones.

Pisces colors: **shades of white and beige, sea green, indigo**

Pisces metal: **pewter**

Pisces flowers: **violet, lotus, iris**

INCREASE YOUR PISCES POWER WITH: orbs, floating candles, incense, bamboo, chimes, bells, sand dollars, shells, starfish, sand gardens, sandboxes, aquariums, fountains, and, of course, fish imagery and actual fish.

ON PISCES' DOMESTIC SOUND TRACK: "Who Will Save Your Soul," by Jewel; "32 Flavors," by Ani DiFranco; "You Can Close Your Eyes," by James Taylor (the Sheryl Crow version, too).

job juju

CAREERS

People who know from the get-go what they want to be when they grow up are among the rarest breed. The overwhelming majority of us take a class in school that sets off a mental lightbulb. Or maybe we meet someone at a party with a fascinating background, answer an ad in the paper, or follow in the footsteps of a family member. And somehow, the bits of information and experience start forming a shape that points in a direction that leads to an interest, a talent, a mission, a career.

Growing up, I had no idea I'd become a horoscope columnist. A movie star! A recording artist! A stage performer! Yes! A horoscope columnist? Nuh-uh. I have to admit it—I'm a classic Leo. My favorite fruit is limelight; my favorite instrument is hands clapping, preferably after I've just taken a bow. These preferences led me first to violin recitals and school plays, and then, as an adult, to summer stock and Vegas lounge show stages. Life was my cabaret, ol' chum! I was making a pittance, with no idea where any of it was going, but as long as I was growing as an artist and a performer, who cared?

And then I moved to Los Angeles, and everything changed. The only performances I was giving were from table to table, as I recited the daily specials and repeated the lunch order back to each customer. I loved meeting people and the social aspect of being a waitress, but unfortunately my balance and organizational skills weren't up to par. I floated from restaurant to restaurant. At best I was tolerated; at worst I was fired. After one particularly brutal beer-in-customer's-lap incident, I found myself not only without a job, but without a clue about how I was going to survive.

That's when a scrap of paper changed my life.

It had a phone number on it. A friend of a friend of my roommate had ripped it off the job board at her community college. It was attached to an employment ad requesting a personal assistant. I called. The woman on the other end of the phone said, "Tell me about yourself." I rambled on for a few minutes, and then she gave me her address and told me to come over. When I got there, she summed me up with a couple of pointed questions, one of which was, *When is your birthday?*

When I replied "August fifth," there was a jerky tilt of her head, like she'd just heard a noise in the other room, and she froze for a moment before saying, almost under her breath, that it was the same day that Sydney Omarr was born on. "Oh!" I exclaimed, as though that meant something to me, which it did not. I wasn't savvy about astrologers at that point, or perhaps I would have known who this woman was.

The next thing I knew, she was handing me the keys to her house and her post office box, and giving me a wad of petty cash as she instructed me to pick up her party dress from the dry cleaner. I remember her winking at me and commenting, as she saw me to the door, "See how much I trust you?"

I worked for her for six months before I figured out exactly what she did. She was Joyce Jillson, a famous astrologer and best-selling author whose life, personality, and way of seeing the world were kooky, colorful, and unlike those of any other person I have ever met. For thirteen years I was her assistant and apprentice. And though I wasn't acting or singing or doing anything onstage, Joyce showed me how I could apply my Leo need for attention to endeavors that were essentially behind the scenes. She taught me to approach every aspect of my job as if it were a performance, and I indeed felt I was a star, even if all I was doing was delivering papers, sorting the mail, or scheduling appointments.

Joyce also helped me understand astrology by explaining it in terms any Leo could relate to. The planets became characters in my imaginary drama, wearing the costume of the sign they were transiting to express their nature, just as an actor wears a costume to portray a role. When the sun is in Leo, he's Liberace—flamboyant, prolific, and creative. When Venus was in Libra, she is Holly Golightly, fabulously sophisticated one minute, wistfully lonely the next. I began to look at life with more levity and playfulness as I actually talked to these characters in the heavens, asking my planetary friends to weigh in on my "issues," tell me about the past and the future, give me more to laugh at, and help me make decisions.

I believe that any sign can be brilliant in any profession. Some professions tend to attract more of one sign—Cancers are often attracted to healing professions, Aquarians tend toward teaching, and Libras are often interested in politics and civil service—but one can also find gifted people of every sign in every profession.

Where astrology can give you an edge is in your approach to your career. Are you a Virgo having trouble with the new software your boss wants you to learn? Reading a manual may seem outmoded to an Aquarius, but for Virgo it's the easiest and fastest way to get up to speed. Are you a Sagittarius who is thinking that a job at another company looks more promising than the one you just agreed to do? Get used to it! For your sign, the grass is always greener in front of the office across the street. Accept that it's in your nature to speculate, and then dive into the job you're doing, intent on finding and exploiting its opportunities for adventure, wonder, travel—all the things you need in a position. Are you stymied about how to ask your Capricorn boss for a raise? Put your request in writing—Capricorn bosses respect formality.

A new moon was in Libra, Joyce Jillson's sign, on the day a small group of tearful friends released her ashes into the Pacific Ocean off the coast of Santa Monica. At the new moon, the moon does a disappearing act, leaving a silent void in the sky. This lunar illusion marks a lucky starting day for projects, relationships, and (on that night, I believed) spirits. Later that night, when I looked up to say goodnight to the stars, I heard the enchanting laughter of my teacher and friend. "On to new dimensions . . . " she sang, as she danced off to join the other characters in the heavenly opera of my imaginings, "and you too, Holiday."

And so it was.

Read on for more clues about how your sign can take care of your own business with cosmic grace.

★ ARIES ★

ARIES AT WORK: It's been said that nice girls don't get the corner office. Lucky for you, when it comes to work, you're no nice girl. Okay, you *have* been known to bring a dozen muffins to the early morning meeting. And you listen kindly to your colleagues' ideas, even when you know they're no good. And you'll stay late without making a stink about it. But make no mistake, your first instinct is to kill the competition—trample 'em with your pretty little spike heels.

FINDING YOUR THING: You're not afraid to try a job on for size. Another gal might turn down a job that's obviously not in line with her career objectives. But you think, *What's the harm? Strawberry-picking might be a fine way to spend a few days.* Answering the phones for a bookie? *Hmm . . . interesting character study!* You don't think it's the slightest bit weird to do a job for a week and then decide it's not for you. You'd rather have that experience for a week than never know for sure what might have been, so your pre-edited résumé is colorful and mind-boggling. But every *No way is this for me* leads you closer to *This is sooo my thing.*

THE LEARNING CURVE: You learn quickly from experience. Furthermore, no matter how much your instructor tells you how to do a job, you won't figure it out until you're the one doing it. So just smile sweetly and say, "Cool" until they hand over the reins.

YOUR SUPERPOWER: passion. Passion is the difference between doing a job and being on a career trajectory. It doesn't matter what your career choice of the moment is, if you feel passionate about it—if you can talk enthusiastically about it until your listener turns blue, if it feels more like a hobby than a profession, if you have to pinch yourself every once in a while over the fact that you're actually being paid—then it's a brilliant choice for you.

FAB JOB IDEAS: activist, ambulance driver, barista, doula, DJ, journalist, real estate developer, reality show producer, soldier, teacher, T-shirt designer, youth counselor

★ TAURUS ★

TAURUS AT WORK: So, you love money. That's (hopefully) the least of your sins. You're working for the tipping point, the win-win, the big *cha-ching*. In the meantime you just might find your specific purpose, or your nonspecific joy, your groovy talent, and your holy grail of goals. So chase the money. And then enjoy what happens at every incremental step along the way.

FINDING YOUR THING: As a grounded individual, you have a general sense early on about how you'd like to make your living, but it takes a while to work this into a niche, so you may bus a few tables and fulfill a few orders to build up the résumé that helps you get to your dream occupation. No problem for you—your work ethic is as solid as your craving for the quality stuff that your paycheck can buy.

THE LEARNING CURVE: You like tasks that have precise guidelines and obvious results. You duplicate well—if they can show it, you can deliver it in that way. And if they can't show it, if the teacher isn't equipped to demonstrate the job at hand, then you'll make up your own way. Right or wrong, they can't say you didn't attempt to do the work.

YOUR SUPERPOWER: results. You see the bottom line. The solution always originates within the problem itself. You understand that when someone hires you, they do it in order to solve a problem. And you do your best to make sure that the problem is not only solved, but also forgotten, as you build into the future.

FAB JOB IDEAS: educator, environmental scientist, lobbyist, lounge singer, music instructor, mystery shopper, pet groomer, road manager, taste tester, veterinarian, voice-over actress

★ At the Zodiac Café ★

Coffee has gone convoluted, wouldn't you agree? With such a bevy of beverages to choose from, you could quiz the barista about the menu board all day. Or how about just ordering a tall cup of something sun sign–specific?

ARIES: Ristretto—the strongest and most concentrated espresso drink. Not for the faint of stomach, but just fine for you.

TAURUS: Oolong—the champagne of teas for the most refined of the signs.

GEMINI: Bubble tea—a perfect conversation-starter for Gemini, the sign most likely to chat with strangers in the drink line.

CANCER: Green tea latte—creamy, jitter-free health in a glass. Easy on Cancer's sensitive system, and nurturing like a warm hug from the inside out.

LEO: Caramel ice-blended cappuccino—topped with gobs of fluffy whipped cream, it's all about the presentation for Leo.

continued...

VIRGO: Spicy chai—a complex flavor for the logistician of the zodiac, who has a fine appreciation for unique blends of flavor and function.

LIBRA: White pearl green tea—distinctive and soft, for soothing your busy mind.

SCORPIO: Macchiato—you'll love the controversy surrounding how it's supposed to be made.

SAGITTARIUS: Dark-roast coffee—Viennese, French, or Italian, appealing to your affinity for all things worldly.

CAPRICORN: A no-nonsense cuppa joe—for a busy sign that doesn't want to waste time or brain cells fretting over which fussy drink to pick.

AQUARIUS: Floral teas, like lavender, rose, or jasmine—BYO pinch of mugwort, which is legendary for inspiring dreams. Aquarius knows that waking dreams are even better than sleeping ones.

PISCES: China black tea—for the Zen master of the zodiac.

★ GEMINI ★

GEMINI AT WORK: Work, shmerk. If it's not fun, it's not for Gemini. Am I saying she has a questionable work ethic? Not at all. Because Gemini can commit. What's more, she can have a ball sweeping the floor. And she can enjoy running the coffee pot just as much as she can enjoy running the company. She's always looking for the amusements in life, and she therefore always finds them. If there is a funny monkey website, for example, that allows you to program a chimp in a wig to say, "The conference call has been moved to three o'clock," Gemini is all over it. That said, when it stops being fun for her, she's the first one out the door.

FINDING YOUR THING: If you haven't found it yet, relax. For Gemini, there is no one thing; there are many things. You're multitalented, and you could keep discovering new interests into the next century. So instead of wondering if you'd be better off quitting this job or going for that position, focus on mastering whatever you're doing now. Once you become masterful, doors open and down from the heavens drop signs that make it absolutely obvious what your next career adventure is going to be.

THE LEARNING CURVE: You're quick and bright, but you're easily bored. You stop learning and improving at the first whiff of the doldrums. You're best in environments that require you to multitask.

YOUR SUPERPOWER: saleswomanship. Business is about sales. Sales is about communication. And communication is your specialty. With a little focused training, you can be an absolute superstar in your chosen career. The best part is that you don't have to take on the stress of running everything in order to feel fulfilled. Did you know that in a lot of companies, the top salespeople earn more than the CEO?

FAB JOB IDEAS: advertising copywriter, beat reporter, freelance photographer, media librarian, personal stylist, preschool teacher, screenwriter, translator, web designer

★ CANCER ★

CANCER AT WORK: The thing about you Cancer women at work is that it's not always obvious that you're working. Sometimes your work looks like lying on the sofa and thumbing through a mail order catalog. Sometimes it looks like sipping coffee and chatting on a cell phone. No matter how it looks, make no mistake: Work is getting done. Cancer likes to let the unsolved problems breathe—with a little space, they just might resolve themselves. And if not, that space leaves room for Cancer's massive intuition and creativity to make it happen, quickly and efficiently. You can't stand to be rushed along or pressured. And you have no problem letting colleagues know when they are cramping your style. With your crabby pincers, you like to nip problems in the bud. But once you've said your piece, you're a pretty laid-back leader, even if the only one you're leading is yourself.

FINDING YOUR THING: You wouldn't dare design a career with your head—you know it would be a waste of energy. Things either feel right or they don't. When they do, you move. And with each move, your career path unfolds before you. You get into one school instead of the other; your cousin puts in a good word for you with her boss; your company is opening a new branch in California. . . . You don't know where it's all going, and that's the beauty of it. It feels great to be useful. And the more useful you feel, the better you're taken care of.

THE LEARNING CURVE: The hardest thing for you about learning a job is that while someone is showing you how to do it, you're already seeing how it can be done better. But if you point this out, you alienate your teacher, and that's not smart. If you can control your urge to take over just long enough to absorb an entire set of instructions, you rock it.

YOUR SUPERPOWER: familiarity. You're so in love with being in your own homey environment that you'd rather not leave it, so you take it with you. The things that make you feel comfortable—your casual sneakers, a perfectly worn-in chair, your mood-music CD, a picture of Mom—and now everyone around you is feeling more comfortable, too. Clients warm up. Colleagues start thinking of you as family. And the stress dissipates.

FAB JOB IDEAS: architect, doctor, energy worker, feng shui consultant, midwife, nurse, organic facialist, picture framer, realtor, swimming school director

★ LEO ★

LEO AT WORK: As fulfilled as you Leos may be by the other areas of your life—your joyous sex life, exceptional hobbies, a devilish hairstyle, the alarming decorating in your house—there is nothing that can substitute for the full-body, electric buzz of doing a bit of killer business. In the wild, the lioness lives to pounce on her prey—indeed, she survives through her ferocious instinct. Likewise, Leo gets positively springy at the scent of a juicy business transaction—be it big business, deep business, corporate business, personal business, or the business of making cappuccino, being a doctor, running the dry cleaner or the mailroom . . . whatever. The transactions that occur in any and all of these circumstances are opportunities for you Leos to proudly receive all the attention as you nail it.

FINDING YOUR THING: Much of the time, you feel like you're already doing your thing, but the rest of the world hasn't quite caught on enough to recognize it as a "thing" yet, and therefore is also slow in coming with the money. And then you hit your stride, everyone knows it, the money flows, and you think, *Wow. What I was doing before wasn't even close.* But that's what everyone loves about Leo—that brave and guileless spirit, without which nothing noteworthy could really happen.

THE LEARNING CURVE: Leo needs incentives to learn, and those incentives are praise, admiration, and more praise, followed by applause.

YOUR SUPERPOWER: vanity. You care about how you look—to your customers, clients, boss, colleagues, the general public. This keeps you in gleaming form as you sharpen your performance against the highest standards.

FAB JOB IDEAS: actor, barista, cardiologist, circuit preacher, commercial director, cruise ship entertainer, event planner, eBay entrepreneur, hairstylist, sales consultant, stage manager, street artist, yodeler

★ VIRGO ★

VIRGO AT WORK: Dontcha hate it when astrologers call you Virgo chicks names like "practical" and "goal oriented"? I can see you rolling your eyes right now. I can also see that you have a beautifully laid-out to-do list folded up in your purse, and that your calendar is open to the correct date, and that the appointments are lined up with appropriate leeway for traffic and other possible snafus, because you hate to be tardy, and hate when others are, too. (Isn't it annoying when people plead, "Oh, the traffic was just the *worst!*" as though that's a valid excuse to be late? Grow up, people! If there's a possibility of a highway slowdown, leave early! The rest of us managed to get here on time! But I digress.)

Sorry, Virgo. I'm now racking my brain to find another way to describe your working self that doesn't mention how gosh-darn practical and goal oriented you are, but I'm coming up with nothing. Because the old saying "If you want something done, ask a busy person" could also go, " . . . ask a busy Virgo." And in spite of your questionable sense of direction, if there's one place you know how to get to, it's the place where you dust off your hands, do a sassy snap, and declare, "Finished," then strut off. "Next!"

FINDING YOUR THING: Though you have certainly had career fantasies, you're often so focused on handling the job at hand that you don't think to wonder what else you might be doing. This contact leads to that job, which leads to a move, and then to the next job, and then one day, like the '80s Talking Heads song, you may ask yourself, "How did I get here?" The answer resonates quickly: *Who cares? There are people to help; there's money to be made and humanity to serve. How much time can we really waste on questions like "How?" or "Why?" when there is so much to do?* Your greatness lies in your ability to stay with what is tangible and real.

THE LEARNING CURVE: You feel deeply certain that you can do a job, or you wouldn't have accepted it in the first place. So learning is pretty much a nonissue. Your quiet confidence, coupled with a laserlike focus on the bottom-line product, helps you figure out all you need to know, quickly and painlessly.

YOUR SUPERPOWER: to-the-second efficiency. Your number one resource at work is your time, and you don't squander it. One hour spent organizing a fabulous paperwork system could save you dozens of hours through the years. And why waste time going for the "little fish" when you could be frying up a seventy-pound salmon?

FAB JOB IDEAS: accountant, book reviewer, calligrapher, dentist, dietician, investment banker, landscape architect, life coach, real estate flipper, surveyor, window washer, upholsterer, video editor

★ LIBRA ★

LIBRA AT WORK: Democracy, collaboration, and group consciousness, rah rah! You don't have to work up any enthusiasm for your work peeps—it's inherent. You marvel at what can be built when everyone pulls together, communicates, and behaves fairly. You're genuinely "united we stand" and "one for all, and all for one." And while there's no "I" in "team," a team without any actual individuals is a disaster in the corporate softball league. My point being, everyone has an ego. Everyone. And if you don't flash yours every once in a while, it's doormat city for you, toots. And even a doormat with ideas, flair, and the ability to pull the room together really stylishly still gets walked on. So go on—I dare you to stand up and distinguish yourself regularly as remarkable. Let your colleagues know that while you're down with the team agenda, you're also a policymaker in your own right.

FINDING YOUR THING: Usually you know what your calling is because you see it. It's in your college professor, an article you tear out of the Sunday paper, or your great-aunt Lucy. Someone else is wearing your calling like an irresistible outfit on a mannequin in the window display of life. You see it and say, "For me, too!" Don't be surprised if you go in and try on the duds and they just don't fit the same as they did on the model. But when it's truly your thing, it will fit even better.

THE LEARNING CURVE: Because you weigh all the optional ways of completing any given task before you decide what tack to take, it would appear to the untrained eye that you are learning at a leisurely pace. What you really are is thorough. You like to know the mechanisms behind processes, and what happens before and after a job leaves your hands. Let no one rush your deliberations.

YOUR SUPERPOWER: saving the day. There comes a time in every Libra's career when the fate of an entire project rests on your shoulders. And then everything goes wrong. Materials are lost in the mail; the printer can't find the order; the main computer takes a dump. You must improvise. But because you've learned all the aspects of your job so well, you're able to pull off miracles.

FAB JOB IDEAS: air traffic controller, art director, florist, foreign diplomat, lawyer, matchmaker, negotiator, politician, postmistress, support specialist, wedding planner, window dresser

★ SCORPIO ★

SCORPIO AT WORK: When you get down to business, regardless of what that business may be (and, truth be told, half the time you're not even sure yourself exactly what all this effort is adding up to), you unwittingly bring a force field around you into being. The townsfolk gather 'round the door and murmur worriedly amongst themselves, *What is she doing in there?* But they dare not interrupt the Scorpio-in-process. It could be dangerous, like waking up a sleepwalker. Wouldn't want to invoke Scorpio's wrath or, worse, delay or prevent the phantasmagoria of financial wizardry, mysterious dealings, and mad creation that is sure to be the product of all this hubbub.

FINDING YOUR THING: Oh, like it's hard? In the manner of Michelangelo's approach to carving stone, you simply eliminate every piece that's not part of the statue of David. What you're left with is your masterpiece. In other words, if you know that you don't want to be a trucker, a cook, or a social worker, then you're three steps closer to your tour de force. Admittedly, this could take a while—it's a big world of employment out there—but a Scorpio is nothing if not resolute.

THE LEARNING CURVE: Scorpio, dontcha hate it when people ask, "How did you do that?" Because you probably have no idea. Your learning process doesn't seem like a process at all. You either know it or you don't—you're either doing it or you're not. Maybe it's through osmosis, or recalling a past life. What you know is, you're in the flow, so who cares how you got there?

YOUR SUPERPOWER: gatekeeping. You say who's in and who's out. And with a mafioso's resolve, you do what has to be done to preserve the dignity of the work "family." Of course it's always more fun for you to hire someone than it is to fire them. But as the sign of death and regeneration, you understand that either way, you're doing the person a big favor. One can't, after all, reinvent oneself until one has been discharged of one's previous incarnation.

FAB JOB IDEAS: beat cop, caregiver for the elderly, detective, documentary filmmaker, EMT, massage therapist, mortician, sex therapist, surgeon.

★ 𝕾AGITTARIUS ★

SAGITTARIUS AT WORK: People who perceive a job as merely a way of earning money to live are, in your opinion, thinking too small. A career is not a series of jobs, it's an expression of your spirit, a metaphor for your purpose on the planet. It's a way to express your philosophy, chase your pleasure, live your aspirations. Therefore, if your job sucks, why show up at all? This is the idea you struggle with on many a Monday morning. Not one to buy into such realities as, say, the electric bill, you have called in sick on a few occasions, with the perhaps unconscious aim of sorting out this quandary between work and soul. Hey, when you're there, you're *on*. You're giving it harder and better and brighter than anyone. And when you're not there, a wise boss should be wondering, *Is she ever coming back?*

FINDING YOUR THING: You're game for trying almost anything. But you might only try it for a day, or an hour—life is too short to waste even a moment doing something that you consider to be a total drag. (Unless, of course, that something pays you enough to afford a trip to that tree house in Kerala, India, that you've been dying to visit.) By the time you're thirty-five, your unedited résumé reads like the Yellow Pages, and maybe by then you still haven't hit on the penultimate employment. But maybe your thing isn't one thing. Maybe your thing is looking for your thing. If that's the case, you've really been doing your thing all along.

THE LEARNING CURVE: You're undeniably a quick study. And even when you don't know what you're doing, you look like you do, which counts too.

YOUR SUPERPOWER: sheer luck. With Jupiter as your godfather, you're the late applicant who ends up with the job, the one promoted to manager-of-all-things because you were showing particularly strong on the day the former manager-of-all-things happened to quit.

FAB JOB IDEAS: dog walker, flight attendant, importer/exporter, personal trainer, photographer, tour guide, traveling saleswoman, yogini/yoga instructor

★ CAPRICORN ★

CAPRICORN AT WORK: For the climbing goat, the career realm is where you are most engaged in the process of life. It's where you can feed your obsession with levels in a clear-cut way. Unlike other areas of life, work always has a goal—moving to the next pay scale or a higher position, being more prolific than the competition, being more productive than you were yesterday. And the ticker tape running through your head stays very much on theme: *Do the best. Be the best. Better your best. Succeed. Rule. Go, go, GO!* Coworkers are either inspired by your Tony Robbins–in-a-skirt

★ SHE'S A CAPRICORN ★

Capricorns have a reputation for being workaholics. But does the diagnosis really apply when one finds work so engaging that it's more like play—or an all-consuming love affair that compels, intoxicates, and offers transcendence? This was how rock 'n' roll's queen, JANIS JOPLIN, saw her work, and her soulful devotion to music swept into her rapture those who witnessed her. Listening to Joplin's voice is like peeking into Pandora's box: All the pain and joy and chaos and beauty in the universe seem to spring out of her whispering screams. Joplin's life was a rebellious lullaby, and she rocked it hard. Ruled by Saturn, the lessons planet, Capricorn women tend to learn quickly the consequences of trying to fit in tend to be harsh. Joplin's credo: "Don't compromise yourself. You are all you've got."

impression or they are intimidated, avoiding you in the lunchroom. It's all the same to you. You'd rather stick with those who are onboard with your desire to win than waste time with distracting elements.

FINDING YOUR THING: Really, it's irrelevant whether a job seems customized for you. You want to rock it regardless. If you are already good at a task, great—you'll succeed quickly. And if you are very bad at it, great—you'll surprise everyone by overcoming the most challenges when you become the underdog who steals the race. And when a janitor shakes his head in pity as he passes by your office three hours after everyone else has gone home, you laugh inside. If only he knew how much fun you're having giving yourself the gift of a competitive edge.

THE LEARNING CURVE: Thorough learning is what makes you a leader. It's not enough for you to know how to do only your own job. You want to find out how things work. You read the manual. You refer to the notes from the meeting. You test your knowledge periodically, ask experts, and of course check out how others are doing the same job. All of this detailed work takes longer, sure, but you're willing to put in the extra hours until you're rock solid in your knowledge.

YOUR SUPERPOWER: presence. You look the part. You adopt the posture of a powerhouse, the glint in your eye of a contender, the confident, slow-breathing rhythm of a mogul.

FAB JOB IDEAS: chef, curator, gem cutter, historian, executive producer, magazine editor, newscaster, occupational therapist, president, school principal, stockbroker

★AQUARIUS★

AQUARIUS AT WORK: Aquarius sets off to work every day with the same goal—to save the world. And if you Aquarians don't believe that your work benefits humanity in some small or major way, it's short lived for you. That's not to say that every Aquarius labors for the Peace Corps or a non-profit, ecofriendly, women's/minorities'/gay-rights organization. Aquarians in every line of work can find the higher purpose of their job. Waitress? You feed the hungry. Insurance saleswoman? You provide the means by which those in dire straights can be rescued. Computer technician? You keep people from going stark-raving mad.

FINDING YOUR THING: Ever the doe-eyed idealist, you enter into each endeavor with the highest hopes that it's your employment nirvana. And when it turns out that your boss is a real person (and not the guru you thought), that your company is not serving the community at the level you think it is capable of, and that your coworkers aren't recycling, well, you're understandably disappointed. But you can always make a

★ ASTROLOGICAL QUESTION ★

"I've been in sales for years, and I've just been laid off again for the third time in two years. I can't get motivated, but if I don't get my worklife on track, I'm going to be in trouble. I'm an Aquarius. Help!"

Don't hit the panic button yet. First, consider that this may be happening to give you the chance to steer your work in a different direction. I'm betting you have talents you've been pushing aside for too long, and they're not going to let you get away with it anymore.

I'm not saying you should abandon your work experience entirely; you can still make money in sales. But you also have an altruistic and creative side, Aquarius, so you have to believe that what you are selling really helps people live better lives. And you have to believe that you, because of your unique assets and talents, are the only one who can sell it the way you do.

Indulge the talents inside you, whether you want to sing, paint, travel, write, or spend your day with four-legged creatures (hey, why not start a dog-walking business?). Once you've done that, you can let them point you toward your unique contribution to the world.

difference where you are, and I believe it's possible to find your true employment nirvana. It's really out there. So don't give up hope.

THE LEARNING CURVE: You're usually so ahead of the learning curve, it's a challenge for you to stay focused when someone tells you what to do. On the rare occasion when you're actually in over your head, you still catch on quickly. You're constantly surprised by what you know that you didn't know you knew.

YOUR SUPERPOWER: technical genius. You find answers with mind-Googling accuracy, text like the wind, and automate the inanimate, and your cell phone seems to always have at least two bars. Every office needs at least one of you.

FAB JOB IDEAS: dancer, inventor, lifeguard, marketing researcher, mathematician, party planner, philanthropist, plumber, poet, potter, special agent, statistician, stunt double, technician

★ PISCES ★

PISCES AT WORK: How anyone can say, "It's just business" is beyond you. It's never just business. The very essence of business is emotional investment—it's why this product sells over that one, or why this person gets promoted or that person gets fired. There is no such thing as commerce without feeling. And knowing this gives Pisces both an edge and a disadvantage. On the negative side, your sensitivity makes you vulnerable to being hurt by interactions that other people wouldn't think twice about. But on the positive side, you are able to connect with your work and let it feed, fulfill, and thrill you. And you also have a sixth sense about how to elevate your boss or your clients to the same level of enthusiasm.

FINDING YOUR THING: You were born knowing what you're going to do. You live the role before you ever get the job, or even the education for the job. That's not to say you won't have employment in different fields, but all the while you know deeply that it's all designed to prepare and perfect you for the work you were always meant for. If ever you feel lost and don't know what direction to take your career in, all you have to do is ask for a sign. Reading the omens is a specialty of yours, and you usually get a clear understanding of what to do next within days of asking.

THE LEARNING CURVE: You know how people walk up to you in department stores and ask you questions because they think you work there? Well, there's a similar dynamic when you're on the job. Others think you know how to do things without their having actually trained you or witnessed you in action. Even you assume that you can tackle whatever comes up. This usually works to your advantage, but sometimes you must face the fact that there are holes in your training, and that you would benefit from filling them in.

YOUR SUPERPOWER: hiring. You can sum up a person's character and experience level in under five minutes, and you know quickly who is perfect for the job. It's almost frustrating to go through the proper procedures and technicalities of hiring, because you see so clearly who is going to work out and who is not.

FAB JOB IDEAS: journalist, magician, market analyst, movie star, painter, psychic, public speaker, screenwriter, swim coach, shoemaker, theologian, therapist, vintner

make your own fortune, cookie

MONEY

My punk-rock accountant, Keith Clark, likes to tell me every year around April fifteenth, "Relax, it's just money."

Yeah, sure. Easier said than done. My friend Melissa, a Virgo (read: fierce sense of fiscal responisibility), recently confessed to me that whatever frenzy she allows herself at the sale rack, she takes back at least half of it the next day. She told me this with a look of penance pasted on her face, as if expecting me to wag my finger at her, judge her, tell her she was courting bad karma and must change her ways.

She is a woman who finds it hard to relax about money. Who doesn't? Her confession was getting no finger-wagging or head-shaking from this corner. "A girl's gotta do what a girl's gotta do," I simply said, and absolved her as only a good friend can.

Okay, so it's not ideal for the department store. But it's a pretty creative way for a Virgo woman to stick to her spending plan and still get the retail therapy she enjoys. Virgos tend to be hard on themselves, and they can't sleep well when they know they've betrayed their own financial plan in a moment of weakness. And now, because of Melissa's little shopping quirk, she can turn around and invest two hundred bucks a month in a money market account she's growing toward her dream of retiring in the foothills of Santa Fe, New Mexico. Now *that* sounds relaxing.

What about you? What financial habits give you a sense of accomplishment? And which ones do you aim to fix? It starts with your beliefs about money. Does it make the world go round? Does it grow on trees? Is it the root of all evil? Or is it, as George Bernard Shaw suggested, the *lack* of money that is the root of all evil?

Our relationships with money are almost as complex and interesting as our relationships with beings that eat and breathe. And every person— indeed, every sign—has different beliefs about and relationships with money, as you're about to read. First, though, let's get one thing clear: *Your stars won't dictate whether you're a billionaire or bankrupt.* But they will give you hints about your earning potential, suggestions about your financial liberation, and directions for planning your fiscal future.

After all, you may not be able to take it with you, but if you could, wouldn't you want it to be Prada?

★ ARIES ★

EARNING: It's key that you ask for more than you think you deserve going into any job. As the first sign of the zodiac, you have huge beginner's luck. Your power is strongest right at the start of every situation. So going in at the right salary clinches your financial success.

SPENDING: You're like that kid at the carnival who blows through the five bucks Mom handed out in the first twelve minutes—wow, does anyone ever knock down those pins and win the big teddy bear? Hardly. Now what? You're forced to use your creativity to have the kind of fun money can't buy. And that's where the exuberant stuff of life awaits. The funny man with the long beard gives you a free balloon. There's a dog-and-pony show and you have front-row standing room. And your sentimental notions about your broke days make your breadwinning days all the sweeter.

INVESTING: Get in and get out. Flipping is your kinda thing—real estate, day trading, craps. But the best investment you could ever make is in your education. You benefit especially from certifications that are not mandatory but that show your range and gumption.

★ TAURUS ★

EARNING: Yes, your work ethic is intact. And yes, you enjoy a good sweat and an aggressive effort once in a while. But you're also keenly aware that there are ways to earn money that require no physical effort at all. And those are for you. So do your research. Risk. Be fiscally forward. It's your mind, not your body, that will make you rich.

SPENDING: You're free with the dollars, that's for sure. But you don't spend on frivolous items. You're into tried-and-true luxuries—a car, a gemstone, or a rare guitar—the kinds of things you're sure will keep their value. It's a bonus when you get a bit of respect along with the pleasure of enjoying what belongs to you.

INVESTING: Commodities are the luckiest. Can it be traded? Delivered? Stored? Does it smack of actual value, perceived value, or potential value? If these questions can be answered affirmatively, you're in. (But whoa, Nelly, don't forget to do your homework, too.)

★ GEMINI ★

EARNING: For you it's not about the money, it's about the deal. You want to know that your efforts have allowed something interesting to occur—something that wouldn't have happened without you. The exchange of energy between people gives you a thrill, regardless of what else is traded in the arrangement. So it doesn't matter if you're selling pencils, closing real estate, or teaching kindergarten. What does matter is the charge you get from a zippy interaction. Now, you can't exactly buy groceries with feel-good vibes, but those vibes do attract money, so it all works out.

SPENDING: Impulsive Gemini, convenience stores were made for you. So were drive-through coffee huts. So were the eye-level shelves in the grocery store that practically require you to grab some gum and check out the latest celebrity gossip. The downside of your spontaneous nature is your slippery relationship with petty cash; the upside is that your free feelings about money keep the channels open for big and small checks to find their way into your account. So it's easy come, easy go, easy come again . . . and so on.

INVESTING: You're just not turned on by smart but safe investments, so you're more likely to take a chance on tech stock than you are to buy government bonds. And if you had $500 to invest in starting a business, you'd spend most of it on a killer outfit to wear to meetings. And you wouldn't be wrong in that choice. Because for you, confidence is the difference between making hundreds and making hundreds of thousands, or millions.

★ CANCER ★

EARNING: Money is relative. What seems like a big salary one year is a pittance another year. What won't buy bread and cheese in one place is considered "mad cheddar" in another city. So you try to not concern yourself with the dollar amount so much as with the value of your overall lifestyle. This balanced approach helps you live well on whatever money you're making. It also helps you ask for more when you need it. Your palms don't sweat, nor does your voice go funny. You're centered on the value you bring to your work, so there's nothing to get uptight about. If they can pay you more, they will. If not, so what? Jobs are like a D train in midtown: You can get off one, and another one will come along ten minutes later.

SPENDING: You're very sensitive. Stress is like a toxic fume to you. So you're a big fan of staying within your means. The nervous tension that goes along with living beyond your means can quickly turn into a health issue. Why put yourself through it? Besides, financial comfort breeds more financial comfort. Your bank account expands when you feel flush and contracts when you feel tight. So lead with abundant feelings, and you get rich.

INVESTING: Don't think, just answer: yes or no? Now go with that answer—maybe even before you know the investment in question. Because your subconscious already knows. And investing for you is best achieved through intuition and instinct. Too much information muddles your initial sense of an investment. Also, as a security-conscious individual, you like the low-risk options, the insured and guaranteed money. There's nothing wrong with a good old-fashioned savings account, and it's best to keep the money there until you feel absolutely sure there's a better place for it.

★ LEO ★

EARNING: Your ideas of what you should be paid are often way above or far below the fair market value. For you, money is just another way to get a rise out of the people around you, whether they're saying, "Poor girl, slaving away for a pittance," or, "Yeesh! That girl's got bank!" For this reason, it's never a bad idea to get someone else—Libra or Capricorn for instance—to negotiate your salary.

SPENDING: Some people get money and then spend it. As a Leo, you often prefer to spend the money first and then find a way to make it. This is how you remain upwardly mobile. Moving into a bigger pad than you can really afford, for instance, pushes you to ask for a raise or find a better job.

INVESTING: You know a sexy product when you see it. It's irresistibly simple, provocatively accessible, ecstatically useful. That's what you're looking for in an investment. Anything too complex or convoluted makes you feel like stashing your money in a hole in the ground instead.

★ VIRGO ★

EARNING: You tend to be modest in your salary negotiations. The going rate, you figure, is going for a reason. Luckily, a good employer will notice and reward your considerable assets when it's time for a bonus, raise, or promotion. Unless they don't. Then you usually make a solid case for yourself and take it a notch higher. Consider learning a lesson from your unreasonable Leo and Sagittarius friends: Just ask for the crazy money up front and see what happens.

SPENDING: Again, the "p-word" comes up: practical. You huff, "Since when is a pair of Jimmy Choos considered practical?" Come on. You know you've worn them enough times now that the amortization of usage figures at a bargain-basement daily price. Nice try, though.

INVESTING: You're good at this, because you're farsighted. You don't mind if an investment isn't going to bear fruit for ten years. Once you commit the money to it, you don't give it too much thought. The one thing that can hang you up is your aversion to risk, which can keep you playing too small a financial game. Don't worry; you can dare to go for the million-dollar idea and still put money in your 401(k) plan.

 ★ LIBRA ★

EARNING: You believe in justice in all things, especially salaries. So the fact that women's salaries are 25 percent less than men's, on average, really gets your goat—or tips your scales, as the case may be. You're an expert at making a case for why you should be paid as much as every Jake, Jeff, and Jerry. But have you made a case lately for why you should be paid *more* than they are? No? Well, maybe it's about time.

SPENDING: It's not the actual purchase, but the romance thereof, that sends you into shopping orgasmia. The way you're treated by the clerk, the care that has been taken in displaying your potential purchases, and the aesthetics of the shop—music, a roomy lounge, scented soap—it all matters if they're expecting you to drop coin. And, if the retail seduction has played out to your liking, drop coin you will. Though you're far more likely to max out the plastic on someone else's birthday gift than on a pair of shoes for your own wardrobe, you usually make up for the personal sacrifices you've endured throughout the year with one big present to yourself for no reason at all (which is, of course, the best reason there is).

INVESTING: Some Libras find it so difficult to decide where to invest that they would rather employ a financial planner to get them sorted out than figure out what to do on their own. Libras are particularly lucky in an investment-club atmosphere, where the social aspect makes financial dealings fun. Mutual funds are a forte.

★ SCORPIO ★

EARNING: Starting salary is minimum wage? No problem. Scorpio is the queen of turning low-wage jobs into million-dollar enterprises. "Everyone has to start somewhere" is your motto. And your big attitude in this regard helps you hoodwink employers into giving you a chance over job candidates who have more qualifications but less conviction. Of course, at some point someone has to cough up the dough, or you walk. And being willing to cut loose a job that's not paying you well is the ultimate negotiating tactic.

SPENDING: You possess an incredible talent—you can get out of Target for less than $15. It's true! Most people go into a grocery store needing three items and come out with three bags full. You buy what you need and then you're out. And this habit carries over into all other financial areas. For instance, when you buy a car, you get only the "extras" you planned on. Your ability to stick to budget—your own or your company's—is rare and cherished. The more money you accumulate, the less you want to spend it.

INVESTING: Whereas you are not into frivolous spending, when it comes to investing, you are willing to take a risk. In fact, you prefer it. You're the sign most likely to make an all-or-nothing bet. Day trading is fun for you. Investing in start-up companies is another lucky option.

★ ♐ AGITTARIUS ★

EARNING: The social aspects of your work are so important that they color your earning potential greatly. You'd rather make less money working with inspiring and fun people than make a load of money working by yourself. And you'd rather lose money than work with someone you can't stand. Employers and clients often mistake your nonchalance about salary figures as a cue that you need more money to get excited about a job. Often that works in your favor.

SPENDING: You do go to extremes, but it always works out in the end. Sometimes you buy in bulk, spending hundreds of dollars on something you'll use all year, like toilet paper or salsa. But look at all you save! Other times you plan to blow a week's worth of grocery store money on one night out with your entourage—until some rich benefactor at the end of the bar covers the tab. And when it comes to retail, your luck is just ridiculous, as you snatch up designer labels at garage-sale prices. But don't rub it in—you'll only make the rest of us mad.

INVESTING: You love spontaneity and have no problem, much to the consternation of your partners, following through on an investment whim. A tip from a friend goes much further than an article in a magazine or advice from your banker. And lucky Jupiter smiles on your gumption. Even when your investment doesn't pay off in dollars, you can point to how it has more than paid off in other ways. And no one can say you're wrong about this. You can't, after all, put a dollar amount on the thrilling life experience you get from chasing things that you can put a dollar amount on.

★ CAPRICORN ★

EARNING: It's not the salary, so much as the power that goes along with the salary, that makes a difference to Capricorn. So you are willing to do something like taking less money if you're working for a large, prestigious entity. Because in doing so, you figure that you're impacting the world in a bigger way than you could by working for a less influential institution and making more money personally. And you always take into consideration the benefits and perks. Health insurance and retirement plans factor heavily, as does potential for upward mobility within a company. In the end, your sacrifices along the way will be more than compensated for, as you can't help but reach the upper echelon of earners in any given situation.

SPENDING: From handbags to houses, you want to know you got the best for the least. So you're cool with your cash. What's the big hurry? You always pay more for wanting things too much, and if there's anyone who can exert emotional control over their desire for stuff, it's you.

INVESTING: It behooves you to set up systems that make it easy for you to figure out your bottom line, because you like to know at any given moment how much money you have to work with. And since you prefer not to do redundant financial chores, you'll find that having your monthly bills, savings, and investments withdrawn automatically from your account is most agreeable. Conservative, long-range investments provide the stability you value.

★ AQUARIUS ★

EARNING: You'll work for peanuts, as long as you are appreciated and the work is in line with your principles. Good for your employer, bad for you. Because lots of times, the people paying you have more than peanuts to work for, but once they find out you'll work for peanuts, they have no incentive to give up the real *dinero*. So do yourself a favor: Get the inside scoop whenever possible. Find out how much the last person got paid, and how much the others are making. And don't feel guilty about making more money. Just imagine how much more you can do for the world with expanded resources.

★ SHE'S AN 𝔸QUARIUS ★

As affable as she is laughable, **ELLEN DEGENERES**'s quick-minded Aquarian energy is the stuff good moods are made of—and that popular appeal and success are driven by. Her rare combination of levity and sense of self has allowed her to tread in tenuous entertainment territory—coming out on television, for instance—without losing her confidence and personal power, as might happen for someone who handles life with more gravity. Her close connection to what's good about humanity, as well as her observational commentary, is pure Aquarius. Think she's telling a joke? She may be, but chances are, there's some hardcore wisdom at the heart of it. Try on some of her brand of intelligence, and it'll likely take you far.

SPENDING: You like to buy things you can eat, wear, or do. And you like a fast computer. Other than that, what's the point? The accumulation of stuff actually grosses you out. Serious inner conflict arises in you when you buy the latest, fastest, shiniest gadget because you think it will change your life, and then it turns out to not be as earth shattering as you'd thought. But that's what eBay and the Salvation Army are for. Most Aquarius women are categorically against storage units, preferring to believe that if you're not currently eating, wearing, or doing the thing, perhaps you shouldn't own it.

INVESTING: The investments that best pay off for you are the ones that you feel create a great deal of goodness for others. And in your book, charitable gifts are financial investments, too—investments in your planet, or in the evolution of humanity. What could be more fruitful?

★ PISCES ★

EARNING: The only jobs worth doing, as far as you're concerned, are the ones you would do regardless of whether you're getting paid. However, when you take that enlightened view into salary negotiations, you may wind up settling for way too low a figure. Make things easier on yourself—use a Capricorn or Libra as a sounding board when you're grappling with the particulars of a work arrangement.

SPENDING: Maybe it's a pair of ultra-skinny jeans or a gym membership you never used. Or maybe it's a weird plot of land in the middle of Podunk Nowheresville. Every Pisces has a few of these purchases that, upon reflection, seem ridiculous. That's because your relationship with money is based on emotions, which means that something that feels like a great idea in the moment sometimes turns out to be a passing mood. Going through your personal belongings is like taking an inventory of past feelings. You remember the lonely mood you were in when you bought those cozy UGG boots, and the happy song in your head on the day you snatched up that polka-dotted chair. You're not overly concerned with getting the best deal, because the karma of a transaction—what the item means to you, what it means to the person selling it, and so on—has more bearing on your decisions than a dollar amount.

INVESTING: Your investments bear fruit in direct proportion to the level of passion, optimism, and goodwill you bring to them. So the most important rule of investing for Pisces is to never make a move unless you're getting that lucky tingling—a buzziness in your head and chest, or a lightness in the tips of your toes. Feel it? Go for it. Don't feel it? Take a pass.

★ destine nations

TRAVEL

Have you ever been to a new place where you felt right at home immediately? As if you had been there before and could almost navigate to the nearest gas station and find the most inviting hotels without asking directions?

Have you ever fallen completely in love with a place? So much so that you wanted to explore its every secret, watch it change colors from dawn to noon to night, and wander its spirals of streets until you knew its geography like a friend? Or did you ever just think a place was wicked cool?

★ I love the way traveling can inspire these feelings in me. My friend Marly had a similar experience on her latest summer trip to Sweden. On a quest for the quintessential kebab stand, she found herself taken in by the bohemian charms of the old-town district of Gothenburg called Haga. One day, she was drinking a Swedish cappuccino outside Café Kringlan when an amorous couple approached her, arms and fingers intertwined, with the bewildered look of honeymooners lost in love—or, it turned out, just lost in general. Tourists. They asked for directions to Lilla Torget, which Marly offered happily with many assurances that they'd love the cobblestone square and its fantastic outdoor eateries. The couple thanked her and turned to go, but before they did, one of them said, "Your English is beautiful. You must have studied for a long time."

She passed for a local. In a very small way, she had *become* one. She had absorbed the place that she loved so much that she had actually become a part of it. Marly was elated.

Now, it could be that a delicious astrological compatibility was to blame for this moment of communion. Just as metaphysicians believe everything is alive—including rocks, buildings, beliefs, and concepts like chivalry and feminism—astrologers believe that everything has a birthday, and therefore a sign, including countries.

A city or country's birthday is usually the day that epitomizes that location's identity. For example, the United States is a Cancer because it celebrates its birthday on July fourth. Cancer is the sign of Mom, baseball, and apple pie. It's the Liberty Bell and mortgage rates, family, and the sacredness of home sweet home.

Patriotism might not fly your flag, however, so maybe a trip to a Virgo country like Chile would be more fulfilling for you. Just like a Virgo person, Chile may appear to be conservative, polite, perhaps even formal, but just under its surface is a wildly passionate spirit. While Chile's duality can remain hidden until you seek it out, a Gemini country like Egypt has a split personality that is readily apparent to anyone who spends time there. Its abundance of opposites—ancient culture and modern amenities, hot days and cold nights, great wealth and severe poverty—gives the country an inherent sense of juxtaposition that evokes the Twins.

Planning any kind of travel, whether it's a long weekend in another part of your state or a globe-trotting gap year, can require tremendous mental energy, and it's natural to feel overwhelmed by logistics and a fear of the unknown. Some people seek out travel agents for help with all the details, but I recommend consulting your sun sign for guidance about your journey. Just as your sign can influence your compatibility with your friends or romantic partners, so can it play a part in the relationships you develop with different geographical locations. If you tap into this awareness before you head off on your adventure, you just might form a lifelong bond with your dream destination.

★ ARIES ★

TRAVEL STYLE: When the impulse strikes, you're ready to get up and go. Unless you have bought tickets or made reservations in advance, however, most times you'll get up and wait instead. Once you arrive at your desired destination, your curiosity drives you to soak up as much of it as you possibly can. Since you usually wind up spending very little time at your actual lodging, and because you'll spend most of that time sleeping, you'd rather skimp on the hotel and use your money for something more exciting. Besides, if a hotel has enough stars to take care of all your needs, some of the adventure is lost. Part of the fun for you is in solving the little problems, like getting a blouse cleaned or finding a battery for your camera.

IDEAL TRAVEL PARTNER: You're brave enough to travel alone, but you have a terrific time going with a Leo or a Gemini, too.

ARIES DREAM DESTINATIONS:

England: From the royalty and pomp of Buckingham Palace to its enchanting villages and country gardens, England brings out the princess in Aries.

★ SHE'S AN ARIES ★

It was a time of transition. A time when bras seemed made for burning. A time when a former *Playboy* bunny could transform into a player on the world stage of politics, philosophy, and philanthropy. GLORIA STEINEM embodied the leadership and warrior spirit of Aries by founding the first national women's magazine run by women—*Ms.* magazine—a globally empowering phenomenon. I met her once, backstage at a Jewel concert. My sister-in-law, a bold Aries-rising herself, marched right up and said, "You have opened so many doors for me. Thank you for the courage it takes to be you." Steinem turned to my sister-in-law and the small group of women in our party and said, "Thank *you*—all of you—for the courage it takes to be *you*." Now that's a leader.

Germany: It takes a lot to impress Aries, but between the opera marathons, beer festivals, football, and Gothic castles, Germany will charm the lederhosen off you.

But don't stop there: You know it—the child inside every Aries would love to see all the amusement parks of the world, including all five Disney resorts.

★ TAURUS ★

TRAVEL STYLE: Wherever you go, your stilo is to do it deluxe—to get not only the best you can afford, but the best you can afford after begging, borrowing, and wheeling and dealing. Because what is the point of staying at a fine hotel if you can't use the spa? And if you can't afford the fine hotel, you can always slum it and still book an appointment at the spa. For you, travel is about being relaxed and luxurious. It's about falling asleep on foreign beaches, flirting with people who don't speak your language, and burning cash like it's kindling.

A note about travel food: As the sign of a healthy—and discriminating—appetite, you love to sample rare and pricey local tidbits. However, your taste buds tend to be rather tame. If a food is an "acquired taste," you probably won't learn to love it in the span of a two-week vacation. But treats like gourmet chocolates, candies, sauces, and teas are mementos that revive the freedom feeling of your vacation once you're home.

IDEAL TRAVEL PARTNER: Virgo and Cancer are your partners in living the good life.

TAURUS DREAM DESTINATIONS:

Greece: The gods and goddesses will speak to you through your fantasies when you stroll the streets of Athens or take a spiritual pilgrimage to the Greek islands.

Ireland: From whale-watching to enjoying classical music festivals, from exploring caves to cozying up at a bed-and-breakfast, Taurus feels at home in this fertile green land.

Switzerland: Inspiration strikes when you stroll down the twisting streets of Stockholm, where medieval buildings stand alongside modern architecture.

★ 𝕲𝕰𝕸𝕴𝕹𝕴 ★

TRAVELING STYLE: Why do people get so uptight about travel? With Mercury as your personal travel agent, you simply can't relate. Mercury is outfitted for speed; the wings on his helmet and his feet have the combined power of a strap-on jet pack. Like Mercury, you're always ready to zip to the next block, city, or continent. No convincing necessary—a moment's notice and a backpack are all you require. In a blink you're flying into foreign territory. Maybe you'll come home in a week, but who knows?

You may stay for a year or two. Curiosity is your tour guide; whimsy is your translator; charm is your international currency.

IDEAL TRAVEL PARTNER: Libra and Leo ensure the adventure you crave.

GEMINI DREAM DESTINATIONS:

Belgium: Crossing the fifty-plus bridges that span the canals of the historical city of Bruges tickles the imagination and is a pleasurable way for you to expend your high energy.

Wales: The magnificent medieval castles, gardens, and parks put you in one of your favorite moods—mischievous and magical.

But don't stop there: The world's largest cities will accommodate your fast pace and allow you to see a full range of sights in one day. Consider Manhattan, London, Tokyo, and Hong Kong—all noisy and beautiful, just like you!

★ CANCER ★

TRAVELING STYLE: It's no secret that you can be a touch agoraphobic. So what you need is a travel idea that is so scrumptious and tantalizing, you hardly notice yourself packing, because you just can't wait to get there. Hint: An all-inclusive tourist trap is not sexy enough—not by a long shot. As much as you are tempted to go somewhere where all your needs will be met and you won't have to think too much, the kind of relaxation you really jones for actually involves mystery, discovery, and invigorating challenge. So get off the bus and away from the mind-numbing banter of the guided tour, and poke your head into a mom-and-pop shop; tramp up the mountain, hot on the heels of a rabbit; or dip into the ocean without the snorkel gear, eyes wide open. Once you get a few exhilarating encounters under your belt, you'll be hooked on this crazy pastime called traveling.

IDEAL TRAVEL PARTNER: Scorpio and Virgo will follow you anywhere in the world.

CANCER DREAM DESTINATIONS:

Holland: Though the windmills and tulips are sure to delight you, the mind-blowing art is what moves you at your emotional core. At the Kröller-Müller Museum, check out the van Goghs, then wander through Europe's largest sculpture garden.

United States: With a July fourth birthday, she's a Cancer, just like you. From the Hollywood sign to the Statue of Liberty and all the mountains and canyons in between, you'll never run out of things to appreciate right here.

New Zealand: Though the Crab is right at home in the perfect surf of the North Island, your horizons will broaden if you take in the South Island's rugged coastlines, primeval forests, and glacier-fed lakes.

★ LEO ★

TRAVELING STYLE: What fire-hearted Leo is looking for when she ventures out is a change of pace. So the question is not whether to stay at a five-star hotel or to camp out on the beach. The question is, where is the wicked drama? And which experience is most different from the ones you've been having lately? If life has been uneventful recently, Leo wants to get lost in a fabulously stressed-out city like New York. If it's been a dry dating season, Leo wants to go where the population boasts nine males to every female—Alaska. If she's been moving too fast, Leo wants to be where she can laze on the beach and worship the sun—Ensenada, Jamaica, the Big Island of Hawaii. . . .

Packing tip: Leos are notoriously inept packers. They secretly want to bring the wrong things because it gives them an excuse to go shopping.

IDEAL TRAVEL PARTNER: Sagittarius and Libra are lucky fellow vacationers.

LEO DREAM DESTINATIONS:

Italy: The vital, brilliant city of Rome is the right choice for the luxury-loving Lion. Lounge poolside. Eat real gelato and real pizza to your inner child's contented bliss. Revel in the art, glorious art. When in Rome, you'll do as the Romans do and feel as content as a cat.

Madagascar: Your Leo spirit is stirred when you observe the endangered lemur and birds of the Tsingy de Bemaraha Strict Nature Reserve.

France: From the perpetual spring freshness of the Cours Saleya Flower Market to the wonderful treasures you'll find at a Parisian flea market, your inner artist will awaken. France will become your lover and your muse.

★ VIRGO ★

TRAVELING STYLE: If you're mentally sorting out your next vacation while lying on a beach during your current vacation, you might be a Virgo. Because for you, planning is half the fun of going places. Virgo's quest for perfection extends into travel life in her desire to secure a fantastic bargain in an ideal location during a glorious weather cycle, and in her adherence to an elegant agenda that includes fine service, scintillating activity, deep relaxation, and pleasurable company. Too much to ask? Naw. Especially not if you've planned it well, right?

IDEAL TRAVEL PARTNER: Capricorn and Scorpio complete your vacation picture.

VIRGO DREAM DESTINATIONS:

Brazil: Brazil is diverse and complicated—in a relaxed way, of course. Does that sound like anyone you know? Brazil offers chaotic sophistication, street parades, Carnival, breathtaking beaches, and exotic Amazonian heartland.

Turkey: The abundant natural beauty of Turkey's beaches and rocky coves is intensely romantic. But it's the whirling dervishes and Byzantine mosaics that will spark a spiritual connection in Virgo.

Crete: On the site of Minoa, the oldest civilization in Europe, Virgo gets in touch with her own timeless soul while strolling through miles of Mediterranean white sand and meditative caverns.

★ LIBRA ★

TRAVELING STYLE: Selfless, agreeable, congenial Libra, let me guess—your last vacation was visiting your out-of-state relatives. Yeah, it's a getaway of sorts, but it doesn't really count. You have to be talked into going somewhere just for you—not where your family lives or where your partner wants to go or where your travel agent thinks would be great. Somewhere you dream up because it intrigues you and speaks to your heart. You deserve it! And you need it. Librans are harmonized by beautiful, tranquil environments—and you can still take your loved ones with you. For you, a vacation just isn't a vacation without someone to share it with.

IDEAL TRAVEL PARTNER: Aquarius and Sagittarius are stellar travel companions.

LIBRA DREAM DESTINATIONS:

Argentina: You'll love the savory food, spicy music, and impressive architecture. And you'll have your glamorous *Evita* moment when you become what's new in Buenos Aires.

Austria: Vienna is a sophisticated and civilized city of romance, where you can share a cup of mélange coffee and a pastry after seeing a world-class opera. The Viennese are friendly, warm, and never pushy (a Libra turnoff).

China: Wonders like the Great Wall and the Forbidden City are positively mind altering. And the historic relics and holy mountains forge new pathways between Libra's mind and heart.

★ SCORPIO ★

TRAVELING STYLE: Your destination choices can be so cutting edge that you're really the only one who understands why you want to go where you do. When everyone is going to Hawaii, you think Vietnam sounds groovy. If your location of choice requires you to get special immunization, take your own water, or wear a money belt, all the better. Your favorite experience while traveling is when you are able to blend into the environment and witness the natives interacting as they would if no one were watching. This is especially thrilling if the behaviors you observe are very different from those of people back home. Since you like to pass unnoticed through a new place, you enjoy traveling alone slightly more than you do with a companion—although you much prefer either of those options to traveling in a group, which you find utterly ghastly.

IDEAL TRAVEL PARTNER: Pisces and Capricorn are your partners in adventure.

SCORPIO DREAM DESTINATIONS:

Bavaria: Bavaria's mystery will continue to haunt your imagination for years after your visit. Explore the birthplace of fairytales, both magical and grim, in the old-world castles, and later have a rowdy time drinking with the locals at a München beer garden.

Norway: Norway strikes you with its colorful array of vivid moods. Majestic cathedrals and snow-capped mountains are interspersed with fjords, beautiful period buildings, and lively, absorbing street culture to charm your Scorpio sensibilities.

Morocco: Open up your third eye in Fez, known as the soul of Morocco. Explore the enchanting passages of this mystical city, and you're transported to another time and place. Rich in tradition, Fez is opening itself up, yet in many ways remains a city hidden behind walls. Sound familiar?

But don't stop there: Consider Vegas, *babeee*. This Scorpio city offers one hot invitation to let your wild bad self loose.

★ SAGITTARIUS ★

TRAVELING STYLE: O wide-eyed wanderer, adventure is your battle cry! There is no terrain too rocky, no city too dangerous, no food too icky, no time zone too difficult to get with—you're on world time. It's in your blood, and nothing can stop you from getting your trip on. Flight canceled due to the storm? That's what trains are for. No money? Tents are beautiful. Travel buddy couldn't make it? Whatever—solo journeys rule! You don't need a plan. You don't even need a destination. Because for you it's all part of the journey of firsthand experience. You want what a library book or glossy pamphlet can't possibly provide—the scent of strange, the rush of raw, fresh excitement as the unknown opens before you.

What is a Sagittarian to do when she can't travel? When she can't get away, not even for a day, a Sagittarius gal like you starts to itch for the next great escape. Rest assured, when it comes to travel, you don't have to go far to go deep. All you have to do is start walking down new paths, knocking on new doors. There's a brave new universe behind the door two houses down. Travel is an attitude. The adventure begins the moment you start looking for the extraordinary.

IDEAL TRAVEL PARTNER: Aries and Aquarius keep up with you just fine.

SAGITTARIUS DREAM DESTINATIONS:

Chile: Paradisical beaches, Jurassic vegetation, gorgeous architecture, grand hotels, sensational cuisine, and beautiful people—a Sagittarian treasure trove of experiences, and so much more than another notch on your travel belt.

Singapore: The jungle animals come alive at night, a fact that you'll find out either by going on a night safari or by checking out the swinging city after dark.

Australia: The outback epitomizes the spirit of adventure that your sign is all about. From alpine training to scaling the Blue Mountains, from wrestling with crocs to racing kangaroos (at least, these are the stories you'll tell upon your return; you're a fantastic embellisher), you'll spend your entire time there breathless and exhilarated. Okay, you might chill out for just a day or two to check out the wineries and cheesecake factories, too.

★ CAPRICORN ★

TRAVELING STYLE: As far as you're concerned, there had better be a pretty good reason to pack your bags. Finding the time to travel can feel like a major chore to you. The truth is, it interrupts your work schedule. It feels frivolous. It throws off the focus of your life. It's a distraction, yet somehow you sense it's an important one. And you're right. Try on some of these reasons for size: Well-traveled people have knowledge that other people don't have. Travel broadens your thinking spectrum and powers your creativity. Travel gives you something to talk about when you're building a rapport with clients. Oh, and how about this one: You need rest! You need a break! You need to see something different! Convinced? Great. Because that's the only hard part. Once your bags are packed and your dog is kenneled, you travel like a dream, maximizing your resources, learning, laughing, and making friends. And who knows? You may even accidentally pick up a little business along the way.

IDEAL TRAVEL PARTNER: Taurus and Pisces follow wherever you lead.

CAPRICORN DREAM DESTINATIONS:

Mexico: Capricorns need a challenge, and Mexico rises to the occasion with lofty mountains, tropical jungles, ominous volcanoes, and landmarks that ancient civilizations left behind to tell the story of their own relationship with the cosmos.

India: You'll be moved by the majestic architecture of the Taj Mahal and swept up by the overwhelming spirituality of the lotus temple in Delhi. You will believe you are learning about this sacred land and people, when really you'll be discovering your own sacred core.

But don't stop there: Check out that high island in French Polynesia called Moorea. It's a honeymooner's Garden of Eden, but don't wait for the perfect partner—go when you need to fall in love with yourself again. It's the place that inspired Charles Darwin to write his theory of evolution, and you'll do some evolving yourself amid the grandeur of unspoiled natural beauty.

★ AQUARIUS ★

TRAVELING STYLE: As a true child of the future, you embrace a global consciousness. Therefore, travel is not so much about being blown away by observing how different people live as it is like visiting your extended family. A bonus feature of this open-minded approach is that you get to feel welcomed wherever you go. You're gloriously adaptable. You follow the "when in Rome . . . " adage and fit quickly into the environment you're exploring. This assimilation shows up in your choice of lodging (as you steer clear of the corporate hotels and opt for the homey B&B); food (you're willing to try the frogs' legs and sweetbreads—a far too poetic term for cow organs, ewww—and anything else that's "authentic"); and activities (you learn more from strolling and chatting up the corner shopkeep than you would from joining the $50 dollar tour). Proof that you're fitting in: Fellow travelers, mistaking you for a local, frequently ask you for directions.

IDEAL TRAVEL PARTNER: Gemini and Aries are game for whatever your whim of the moment may be.

AQUARIUS DREAM DESTINATIONS:

Finland: It's eclectic, like you. One day you're in the mood for high art, and Finland says, "Sure!" The next day you'd like to go fishing, and Finland says, "Can do!" It can do nature, it can do cosmopolitan, and, as a bonus, it can do every conceivable form of winter sport.

Russia: The complexities of Russia are endlessly intriguing to you. The museums, which boast exquisite masterpieces by the world's greatest artists, are a thrill. And the inimitable baroque architecture of St. Petersburg is as unique and individual as you.

Ethiopia: The breathless Blue Nile Falls are the ultimate expression of "water-bearing."

★ PISCES ★

TRAVELING STYLE: You travel every day in your mind. Your daydreams take you to exotic and wonderful locations where the conditions are perfect and the people treat you exactly as you prefer. When it's time to actually transport your body from here to there, the logistics of real life can be a shock. You're suddenly expected to deal with niggling details, such as boarding passes and whether you remembered deodorant— hmm . . . that wasn't in your fantasy. The solution? A stellar traveling companion. The right personality by your side, laid-back yet definitely type A, will make the difference between a dream vacay and a wish-you-never-left-home vacay. And if you can't find the travel buddy, the key for you is having the perfect plan. When you've done your travel homework and know where you're going, how to get there, and what you'll need, you can relax and let the wonders unfold.

IDEAL TRAVEL PARTNER: Cancer and Taurus are delightful company.

PISCES DREAM DESTINATIONS:

Egypt: True to form, you channel colorful characters as you journey through Egypt. So, you're Cleopatra as you drift down the Nile, you're a queen in her pyramid home, and you're the Egyptian goddess Hathor, losing yourself in the music and dancing of Cairo's nightlife.

Portugal: Twenty centuries of history, and the fresh Atlantic breeze will blow gently into your romantic soul.

Tunisia: Are you wandering the desert in a BC era, or are you exploring the terrain of a planet in a galaxy far, far away? Gladiators, camels, and hidden geographic surprises make this North African adventure unforgettable.

come as you are

PERSONAL STYLE

My poor mother.

Her conservative upbringing didn't prepare her in the least for a fashion-forward, dress-to-shock Leo daughter growing up in the '80s. I would emerge from my room dressed in men's boxer shorts, ripped lace leggings, five chain link belts, an armful of bangles, an Adam Ant mask of black eye shadow, and hair teased a good eight inches from my scalp. I thought I looked, like, totally new wave awesome. She thought I looked, like, totally mad clown insane asylum.

That's a Gemini for you. Even a Gemini whose own high school wardrobe consisted of a Catholic school girl uniform, plaid skirt two inches below the knee, starched white blouse, and spotless oxfords has a soft spot for trends. However outrageous my get-up was, she reasoned that if it was en vogue, why argue? Fighting fashion is, after all, tantamount to standing in front of a tidal wave with your hand held out, yelling "Stop!"

Looking back on the big hair days makes some wince, others laugh, but not me. I am still proud of my ability to tease and spray hair into a fluffy pile that could house a family of midsized gerbils. I'm proud of my endurance level in relation to impossibly pointy stilettos and my carefully honed skill of navigating a leg into stockings that are ripped in twenty places. In fact, I still have a pair of my vintage ripped lace leggings, which just happen to be back in style—who's laughing now?

OK, but the truth is, my shock dressing never was about fitting in or doing what the other kids did. True to my Leo form, it was about one thing, and one thing alone: attention. I loved to know that when I walked down the hall, people noticed. I loved to be singled out for a little good-natured teasing by the math teacher. I loved to make the jocks laugh and the squares point and whisper. What might have been, to another teen, mortifying was for me fortifying.

Which brings me to ask you—and I have to ask—are you a fashion disaster? That is to say, are you on automatic pilot when it comes to outfitting your life? Have you been parading in around in sweat pants when you could be dancing through your day in an adorable babydoll dress? Or vice versa—are you giving in to the pressure to get dolled up when you really would prefer to kick it in flip-flops and a hoodie? Are you a Sagittarius smothering inside of an out-of-season sweater when you could be tying on your lucky bikini top? Are you a Capricorn who hasn't yet embraced the liberation of a pin- striped suit? If so, consider this your invitation to stop playing it safe, and start playing it planetary. Because some of the most brilliant style decisions are drawn not while looking in the mirror but while looking inward, and looking up.

Oh, stop fretting, you Scorpio women who don't want to wear fishnet stockings. Although I think fishnet stockings might become you, this chapter is not about telling you what to wear. Not entirely. It's about giving you a new frame in which to view your style choices. Because maybe there's something deeply ingrained in you—some cosmic predisposition—that wants to be expressed. Entertaining the idea could, at one extreme, be the start of your own fashion revolution. At the other extreme, it could be the idea that helps you break out of a fashion rut. Or simply nudges you into the perfect outfit for that party you're going to on Saturday night.

Of course, personal style doesn't end with your clothes, so I've included some delicious tidbits about other areas where you can exert your own cosmic taste: your special scent, mode of transport, and communication style, for starters. These are best used not as dictates but ideas to add to your arsenal of personal expression—tinkering tools to take you to the shimmering, confident creature you were always meant to be. Because there are no small choices—not in a life as big as yours.

★ ARIES ★

ARIES STYLE IN A WORD: confident.

IT'S ALL ABOUT THE: silhouette. What do you look like from a distance? What do you look like when you blur your eyes so the details go fuzzy? What is the overall effect? You realize that the bulk of people you run into are going to get a feeling about you, and that it starts when you're still in their peripheral vision. The total image, not the details, is what they'll remember. So your best collection of style choices is crisp and simple, with lines that convey the strength, energy, and vibrancy you prefer to emit.

THREADS: As the warrior of the zodiac, you sometimes think of your clothing as a uniform. It pleases you to know what goes with what. When you come across something that works for you—that makes you feel empowered, appropriate, and attractive—there's comfort in duplicating the outfit exactly, from earrings to socks, whenever you need that feeling again.

LUCKY FASHION PIECE: the red dress. Evocative of the rapturous passion of your ruling planet, Mars, the red dress stirs souls and inspires poetry and song.

STYLE ESSENTIALS: anything to do with exercise. Stuff that makes working out fun, from iPods to instructional DVDs. After all, the best accessory is a bangin' bod.

STYLE EMBELLISHMENTS:

Scents: cinnamon, ylang-ylang.

Makeup: sweat-resistant mascara.

Spa Splurge: aroma stone therapy—rock out and relax all at once.

HOW YOU EXPRESS YOURSELF: directly, with words that cut to the chase. Aries is also quick to pick up on verbal shortcuts and Internet lingo, not because it's cool, but because it saves time. Aries likes other people to be equally succinct and on point. So don't be offended when Aries prompts you with an AYTMTB ("and you're telling me this because . . . ?").

HOW YOU ROLL: fast. Wear a helmet. Whether it's Rollerblades or race cars, the best, in your book, is also the speediest.

GET YOUR PARTY ON: You don't need a reason. Life is for celebrating. Anyway, you work hard, so it follows that you should play hard. Your way is to start with a party of one. If others join in, fab! If not, who cares? You're good company! Your ideal party would be a semiformal event where you're being toasted for a fantastic accomplishment. Second to that, friends getting together to clink glasses at the end of the workweek will do just fine.

ARIES CELEBS GOT PERSONAL STYLE: Gloria Steinem, Aretha Franklin, Sarah Jessica Parker, Erica Jong, Diana Ross, Emmylou Harris, Doris Day, Bette Davis, Mary Pickford, Joss Stone, Loretta Lynn, Liz Phairr.

★ 𝕿AURUS ★

TAURUS STYLE IN A WORD: luxe.

IT'S ALL ABOUT THE: label. Not because you're a snob, but because you value quality, and you expect a high level of workmanship from certain name brands. Of course, you realize that ultimately, style has no brand name—it's an attitude, a series of choices, an emotion that you can create regardless of the name on a label. But somehow the name on the label makes it that much easier.

THREADS: Sensuality is your guiding principle. You like clothing that's so soft, it melts at your touch. You want a fit that's more comfortable than nudity. And you want form that's versatile—clothes so effortless that you could wear them lounging on the couch, but so comfortable that you could wear them to a wedding. All these demands make it challenging to shop. If only you could get away with some kind of feminine equivalent of Hugh Hefner's wardrobe.

LUCKY FASHION PIECE: a necklace. Ever hear of chakras? In yogic philosophy, chakras are energy centers in the body that connect the spiritual and physical worlds. Taurus is associated with the throat chakra, which governs self-expression. And this chakra loves to be adorned with blingy bobbles or precious stones as a reminder that you have something to voice, in your own gorgeous manner.

STYLE ESSENTIALS: a handbag that looks like a gazillion dollars. Better yet, a handbag that actually is a gazillion dollars.

STYLE EMBELLISHMENTS:

Scents: violet. Zeus believed this was the finest flower and named it after his love, Io.

Makeup: Liquid blush gives you that "I'm in love" look all the time.

Spa Splurge: blinged up mani and pedi—but no so gaudy as to compete with your other rocks.

★ SHE'S A 𝕿AURUS ★

SOFIA COPPOLA made her film debut as a baby boy in her father's film *The Godfather* and has been showing up the big boys ever since. Whether competing as a designer in the cutthroat world of fashion or taking home an Oscar for her writing of *Lost in Translation,* she always leads with an indie spirit that elevates her projects to pop culture icons. Here's the secret that Taurus women know innately: Often, making fashionable and creative choices is not a matter of taste, but a matter of integrity. A choice either feels right, sensual, tangible, real—or it doesn't. And Taurus women are far too stubborn to compromise when it comes to something as life-alteringly important as art.

HOW YOU EXPRESS YOURSELF: You like to get your message across with a musical tone. Sometimes it's just a sexy lilt in your voice. Other times it's a mix tape or a song you make up that encompasses your feelings.

HOW YOU ROLL: Taurus is into cars. Classic cars, expensive cars, foreign cars, fast cars—your appreciation runs deep and wide. As for your own car, you like to figure out what the absolute best car you can possibly afford is, and then get one that's slightly more expensive.

GET YOUR PARTY ON: The most important part of any party, as far as Taurus is concerned, is the food. (Conversely, wherever there is fabulous food, there's a party—even if it's a party of one.) Party food is ideally something you wouldn't think to eat at home, either because it takes too long to prepare or because it's too expensive to eat every day. It doesn't have to be uberfancy, but it has to be delectable.

TAURUS CELEBS GOT PERSONAL STYLE: Shirley Temple, Shirley MacLaine, Barbra Streisand, Renée Zellweger, Carol Burnett, Penélope Cruz, Candice Bergen, Martha Graham, Cher.

★ GEMINI ★

GEMINI STYLE IN A WORD: now.

IT'S ALL ABOUT THE: timing. As far as Gemini is concerned, timeliness is the essence of style. The twins can't get their head around how anyone can say, "That piece is timeless." No matter how fantastic a piece may be, if it doesn't feel of-the-moment, it's not, in Gemini's opinion, a fashionable choice. Wearing white shoes after Labor Day, or failing to adhere to the color and fabric schemes of the season, is only the tip of the iceberg.

THREADS: trendy, but not fussy. Flirty, but not slutty. Fun, but not cheap. A bonus for Geminis is that you're able to wear clothes that on others would appear age-inappropriate or give the impression that someone is trying too hard. On you, this clothing just looks fresh.

LUCKY FASHION PIECE: up-to-the-minute tennis shoes.

STYLE ESSENTIALS: a beyond-fabulous phone that does everything but your laundry.

STYLE EMBELLISHMENTS:

Scents: Lily of the valley is an uplifting floral fragrance for Gemini. You're a breath of fresh air, so keep your scent light.

Makeup: Nail polish accents your expressive hands—so, even as you're wildly gesticulating in the air, all they'll notice is your lovely manicure.

Spa Splurge: Chardonnay Sugar Scrub.

HOW YOU EXPRESS YOURSELF: "So yesterday" is so yesterday. Gemini makes an effort to stay hip in all ways, including verbally. Likewise, gossip that's more than twenty-four hours old is eyeball-rolling stale.

HOW YOU ROLL: zippy. Come on, admit it. You have at least one friend who won't ride in the passenger seat of your car while you're driving. And when it comes to dialing and driving, you're notorious. Your safest mode of transportation is a train, where, unlike in an airplane cabin, you can use your cell phone freely or chat up your fellow passengers. And nobody will argue with you about what you consider a safe driving distance between you and the car ahead of you.

GET YOUR PARTY ON: Big events are your specialty. If they have a hundred moving parts—catering, entertainment, dancing, public speaking, a clown—all the better. You find that when you bring groups together, the crowd creates its own kind of order amidst the celebratory chaos. And that's the party magic that keeps you perpetually looking forward to your next mad bash.

GEMINI CELEBS GOT PERSONAL STYLE: Priscilla Presley, Stevie Nicks, Kylie Minogue, Melissa Etheridge, Marilyn Monroe, Sandra Bernhard, Joan Rivers, Nicole Kidman.

★ CANCER ★

CANCER STYLE IN A WORD: romance

IT'S ALL ABOUT THE: mood. You can wear and say absolutely anything, as long as you are in the mood to wear it and say it. Being en vogue means making the right choice based on the vibe you're feeling. On a mysterious, complicated day, the basic black turtleneck that inspires you to snap your fingers like a Beat poet is totally you. And on another day, the springy eyelet baby-doll dress that you wear while lounging on a porch swing and sipping mint tea is also totally you. You are, as Chaka Khan belted out, *every woman*. You truly inhabit whatever costume you've donned for the day.

THREADS: Use your wardrobe to enhance your luminosity. A shimmering beach shell on a chain, opalescent color choices, fabrics that play with the light like water does . . . there's no apparent formula to your style madness, yet somehow it all comes together in a soft, romantic statement. Your tried-and-trues are pure comfort: velour, cashmere, 100 percent cotton.

LUCKY FASHION PIECE: boatneck top. This French neckline is the essence of simple, elegant scrappiness—gamine, playful, unpretentious. It presents a neat balance between the shoulders, front, and back. Its message is versatile: It suggests fun at the boat show, coolness at the jazz concert, or friendliness at the grocery store.

STYLE ESSENTIALS: Cleavage-enhancing underpinnings, seashell jewelry, silver jewelry, mood rings, or moonstones—anything that emphasizes the décolletage adds to Cancer's allure.

STYLE EMBELLISHMENTS:

Scents: Vanilla is a favorite, reminiscent of Mom's baking.

Makeup: shimmer powders and lotions.

Spa Splurge: Hydrotherpay—a blast of H2O to set you right with the world.

HOW YOU EXPRESS YOURSELF: honestly. Pretension really irritates you. You understand people's meaning very clearly, so it's almost insulting when they don't just say it outright. What you need to know is that some people don't want you to be honest with them all the time. And some people don't want you to be honest with them any of the time. For these types, your quiet empathy will be a better gift than anything you could verbalize.

HOW YOU ROLL: *Really? I gotta leave the house?* Video conferencing was made for you. You're better off investing in a computer than a car—go for a state-of-the-art laptop rather than in the hottest wheels to hit the road. But when you really must go, you're not extremely particular about the mode of transportation, so long as it has a heater, an air conditioner, and a comfortable seat.

GET YOUR PARTY ON: When you want to create some social magic, all you have to do is make like Dorothy—click your heels and repeat, "There's no place like home." You love cooking for your peeps, especially because some of them claim they've been healed by your culinary genius. Your second choice is potluck. Your third is takeout. Your 756th is going out.

CANCER CELEBS GOT PERSONAL STYLE: Juliette Lewis, Meryl Streep, Liv Tyler, Courtney Love, Princess Diana, Camilla Parker Bowles, Ginger Rogers.

 ★ **LEO** ★

LEO STYLE IN A WORD: dramatic.

IT'S ALL ABOUT THE: hair. Your hair is your mane, your crown, your self-esteem indicator. Altering the way your head is framed changes your point of view, as well as how people view you. Deep down, you believe that when you change your hair color, sweep your bangs to the left, or pull a hood over your head, you're affecting your destiny. Thus, wearing a ponytail instantly changes the role you are playing in life, which puts you on a different path. So of course you're particular about it. A bad haircut can make you cry like a baby. A good one can empower you to take over the world.

THREADS: There are clothes that people wear, and then there are clothes that wear people—so bold, bright, or unusually designed that the average person would be overshadowed by the dazzle. Leo, however, can pull off these looks. So don't worry if you're inexplicably drawn to these clothes—sparkle-fests or costume-esque pieces that others would feel ridiculous in—because they look completely natural on you. In fact, you look unnatural when you're not wearing something that's a little over the top.

LUCKY FASHION PIECE: a cape. And if it just so happens that capes aren't your thing, then something that makes an equally memorable statement, such as a blue wig, a dress with an impossibly long train, or seven-inch heels, will suffice.

STYLE ESSENTIALS: hats, hair accessories, pendants that hang over your heart.

STYLE EMBELLISHMENTS:
Scents: citrus, especially orange.

Makeup: Self-tanner and bronzer enhance your sun-kissed glow without damaging your skin with nasty UV rays—Love Cat without a tan is like a tiger without stripes.

Spa Splurge: Custom-sprayed Mystic Tan—for the times when you don't have time to properly worship your ruling body.

HOW YOU EXPRESS YOURSELF: with flair. Theatricality is not just for the stage. Presentation counts in all areas of communication, whether you're inviting people to a party you're throwing, having an intimate conversation, or making a public announcement. You are naturally prone to delivering your message in a way that's as attention getting and individualistic as you are.

HOW YOU ROLL: with a posse. Motorcycles and two-seater sports cars are out of the question. You need room for passengers.

GET YOUR PARTY ON: Your ideal fete is lavish, complete with a butler greeting people at the door, professional dancers to set the mood on the dance floor, and fire-eaters to stave off dull moments. A more realistic option is a family party with lots of kids, who can help you fill in the blanks with your imagination.

LEO CELEBS GOT PERSONAL STYLE: Helen Mirren, Kate Bush, Lisa Kudrow, Hilary Swank, J. K. Rowling, Martha Stewart, Lucille Ball, Madonna, Mae West.

★ 𝔙IRGO ★

VIRGO STYLE IN A WORD: elegance.

IT'S ALL ABOUT THE: subtle detail. Nothing is accidental, least of all the things that seem accidental. The careful arch in your eyebrow is as deliberately orchestrated as your day planner. Furthermore, Virgo is fond of creating a signature look. Think Pink's bright hair, Sophia Loren's glamorous glasses, and Raquel Welch's sexy wigs. Maybe it's something as simple as a scarf tied around the belt loop of your trousers, or a charm on your bracelet—there's always a pièce de résistance, a final touch that says you care.

THREADS: A flawlessly executed outfit means you're prepared for anything, even unpredictable, unpleasant elements (stress, weather, and overtime). Wide-legged trouser pants, a crisp white French-cuff shirt, or a figure-hugging jacket give you the versatility to mix it up in a flash. Quality designer threads communicate the competence you exude . . . and want to attract. Nothing about you is second rate, including your clothes.

LUCKY FASHION PIECE: an off-the-shoulder sweater. It sustains the precarious balance between poise and flexibility, character traits that are equally strong in your ruling planet, Mercury. Modest, with a smidgen of suggestion, the sweater communicates accessibility while offering more to the imagination than to the eye.

STYLE ESSENTIALS: smart color-block scarves, kidskin leather gloves, silver and gold hoops for your fingers and ears.

STYLE EMBELLISHMENTS:

Scents: lavender.

Makeup: eyebrow pencil and quality tweezers—don't leave home without them.

Spa Splurge: Japanese Silk Booster Facial—puts the perfection in your complexion.

HOW YOU EXPRESS YOURSELF: Your natural impulse is to do what so many others wish they could—think first, communicate second. After all, if one is to be considerate, one must consider. The result is that you usually hit the perfect tone as you deliver a message that is appropriate to the situation. Here's something else to consider: It might be fun to be inappropriate too, even if that means pushing yourself out of your polite comfort zone. Sometimes that's the only way to convey the passion, humor, and humanity that connect you with others.

HOW YOU ROLL: Who needs a sense of direction when you have a map? Efficiency is your rule of thumb. You're a one-stop shopper, hitting all the errands on your list at once. Convenient, predictable subway trains thrill you—you self-organize with their trip planners and maps. And you're doubly thrilled when you discover a better, quicker route.

GET YOUR PARTY ON: No one throws a spa party like you. A mani-pedi extravaganza, besides creating a relaxing, fun social atmosphere, has the added benefit of allowing you to check "Get manicure and pedicure" off your list.

VIRGO CELEBS GOT PERSONAL STYLE: Raquel Welch, Michelle Williams, Pink, Twiggy, Claudia Schiffer, Faith Hill, LeAnn Rimes.

 ★ **LIBRA** ★

LIBRA STYLE IN A WORD: smart.

IT'S ALL ABOUT THE: first impression. You like to make sure that the snap judgment people are known to make in the first five seconds of meeting you is not only favorable, but impressive. You carefully consider the social cues of your chosen scene before you dress, because a fashion faux pas could prevent you from making the right connections—business and otherwise. You wouldn't wear a miniskirt to a funeral, or business attire to a soiree. You read the invitation. You inquire about the dress code, custom, and style of a place. You give the mirror your signature once-over. Then you walk right in with the majestic presence of a goddess.

THREADS: Thrown together or polished, you make it look so easy. You downplay efforts made and time spent in front of the mirror, because you know, while others may not, that even "thrown together" is a look. You're especially smashing in fabrics that hug the body.

LUCKY FASHION PIECE: the little black dress. That versatile, flattering wardrobe piece is functional in a flash. What other wardrobe item gives you the mileage to turn business meetings into romance in one hip swish? And it gives you the intellectual credibility and style expertise that people expect of you.

STYLE ESSENTIAL: Diamonds are a Libran's best friend.

STYLE EMBELLISHMENTS:

Scents: rose and raspberry.

Makeup: a powder compact—preferably an ornate and expensive one.

Spa Splurges: Ayurvedic massage—sets your searching soul at ease.

HOW YOU EXPRESS YOURSELF: graciously, sweetly, diplomatically. It's your strategic plan to earn trust and rapport—for once you've got that, whatever else you want is a done deal. So you let the flattery fly without a care about how you'll be received. You instinctively know that even if your subject doesn't quite buy the compliment, the fact that you think they are worthy of flattery in the first place will win huge points.

HOW YOU ROLL: Driving stresses you out. Rush-hour traffic in particular can upset your delicate nervous system, so that by the time you arrive at your destination, you feel like you need a nap. Whenever possible, you like to walk or bike to where you're going. But your favorite is when there's someone else driving you; car conversation is intimate and relaxing, so a passenger seat in a luxury sedan is your ride of choice.

GET YOUR PARTY ON: What's the ultimate party for a Venus-ruled Libran lover of love? A wedding, of course! Your own is something you've dreamed of since you were old enough to pull Mom's negligee over your head and call it a veil. Next to that, a friend's wedding is the penultimate affair. You revel in the minutia, from the shade of icing on the cake to the font of the thank-you cards months later. You'll likely be the one who gets a million phone calls that start with: "What should I do about the . . . " and you'll never tire of lending genius advice.

LIBRA CELEBS GOT PERSONAL STYLE: Gwyneth Paltrow, Gwen Stefani, Barbara Walters, Olivia Newton-John, Moon Unit Zappa, Linda McCartney, Donna Karan, Lorraine Bracco, Neve Campbell.

★ Scorpio ★

SCORPIO STYLE IN A WORD: sultry.

IT'S ALL ABOUT THE: mystery. Glamour is an illusion—a trick that draws attention to the things one wants to reveal, and away from the things one wants to conceal. You adorn yourself and behave in a manner that skillfully tells people what you want them to know about you, while maintaining the privacy you so prize. Nothing turns you off faster than someone who leaves nothing to the imagination, in their dress or their behavior. You aspire to do the opposite—to tease, create intrigue, and never give up your secret.

THREADS: Sexy is unavoidable for Scorpio. You could be covered from head to toe, with your figure hidden under an Elizabethan skirt the width of a hallway, and you'd still be considered a tad risqué. In fact, the more demure your choices are, the sexier you become. So go ahead and choose the buttoned-up collar, the long crocheted sweater with the sleeves down to your knuckles, the knee-high boots—whatever makes you feel protected.

LUCKY FASHION PIECE: killer stilettos.

STYLE ESSENTIALS: ultra-hot undergarments, stockings with garters, an Asian fan, a long cigarette holder, a lorgnette.

STYLE EMBELLISHMENTS:

Scent: vetiver, a musky essential oil used in many exotic perfumes. Indian poets praised it as "the smell of the first monsoon shower on parched soil."

Makeup: red lipstick.

Spa Splurges: Sea Salt Scrub to return you to your essential self.

HOW YOU EXPRESS YOURSELF: with innuendo, using as few words as possible. You're a big fan of greeting cards that say it for you and don't allow the recipient to get too far into your psyche. You also like to send anonymous messages and gifts. And then there's the occasional prank call—come on, we know it was you.

HOW YOU ROLL: surprisingly. Your favorite is when nobody sees you coming or going. You pop in and catch others off guard, while you're completely in control. And you leave whenever you want. It's downright sexy, the way you slip out of parties without saying goodbye, leaving people to look for you. As for your mode of transportation, if you've done your job right, what does it matter?

GET YOUR PARTY ON: One-on-one is fun. Intimate adventures are your specialty. It's so much easier to celebrate your relationships when you're in an atmosphere that supports individualized attention. It's not that you fuss over the surroundings or make a lot of specific plans—the quality of your attention *is* the plan, one you know you can execute beautifully. When others are alone with you, be they family members, friends, or romantic connections, they feel like the most important people in the world.

SCORPIO CELEBS GOT PERSONAL STYLE: Kelly Osbourne, Julia Roberts, Winona Ryder, Grace Slick, k. d. lang, Vivien Leigh, Tatum O'Neal, Sally Field, Maria Shriver, Joni Mitchell, Bonnie Raitt, Grace Kelly, Veronica Lake, Meg Ryan, Jodie Foster, Björk, Scarlett Johansson.

★ＳAGITTARIUS★

SAGITTARIUS STYLE IN A WORD: exotic.

IT'S ALL ABOUT THE: journey. If a Sagittarius is asked to choose between shopping and wearing, the shopping wins, no contest. The fun is in finding the perfect piece that will blend in with and give new life to what you already have. You also love trying a whole new look, discovering a different way to be seen in the world. If your style selections also happen to feel comfortable, fit like custom designs, and work brilliantly with what you've got on your agenda, well, those perks are just the cherries on top of your fashion experience.

THREADS: You have high expectations for your wardrobe, expecting it to be as witty and transcontinental as you are. You've been known to create impossible ensembles, like a French-inspired chapeau with a bangle from the Bahamas and an Italian scarf—and you own them like they're the new dress code for the Sagittarian Nation. Call it Sagittarian-ese, with the emphasis on "ease."

LUCKY FASHION PIECE: a bikini! It's the ultimate in no-nonsense—it's scanty, but it offers support where it's needed. True confidence means having nothing to hide, which is why this summertime classic has strong connotations: adventure, athleticism, luxury, leisure, attitude. If your self-esteem is in need of a boost, willful wearing of a bikini top could force you into the right mind-set to conquer the problem.

Historical sidebar: Engineer Louis Réard unveiled his two-piece bathing suit creation in Paris in 1946, four days after the U.S. military set off the first test of the H-bomb near the Bikini Atoll—hence the name. It took another fifteen years for the fashion to take off in America.

STYLE ESSENTIALS FOR SAGITTARIUS: Ready-to-pack clothes that scrunch up small and never wrinkle; sporty pieces that breathe. Indestructible and lightweight bags, leather luggage tags, hiking boots, anything with international flair.

STYLE EMBELLISHMENTS:

Scent: orchid.

Makeup: Kohl eyeliner worked for Cleopatra, and it works for you.

Spa Splurges: Mud Bath—as the most adventurous sign of the zodiac, you might even try it with a group.

HOW YOU EXPRESS YOURSELF: in many languages. Even if you speak only one, you actually communicate in several, because you meet people on their own wavelength and match their verbal style. So you can speak teenager or corporate lingo, you can do grandparent-speak and girlfriend-gab with equal aplomb. And when it comes to putting your message on paper, you're as comfortable with a formal business letter as you are with a sexed-up Post-it note for your beloved.

HOW YOU ROLL: often, in whatever will get you there. Rent-a-wreck, rickshaw, or race car, it's all the same for you. The adventure of a world rushing by you, proof that you're going somewhere, means so much more than your comfort or the style statement you're making en route.

GET YOUR PARTY ON: Every party is a world unto itself. You wouldn't dream of declining an invitation to explore a whole world, now would you? So if you're reasonably sure to meet new people and you have no better offers, you're totally there. When it's your turn to host, you see this as a mind-expanding opportunity for your friends. You introduce new flavors and plan colorful and exciting party features that will make yours a celebration to remember.

SAGITTARIUS CELEBS GOT PERSONAL STYLE: Tina Turner, Caroline Bessette Kennedy, Bette Midler, Tyra Banks, Betty Grable, Christina Aguilera.

★ CAPRICORN ★

CAPRICORN STYLE IN A WORD: classic.

IT'S ALL ABOUT THE: statement. Clothes tattle. They whisper, *I weekend in the Hamptons.* They declare, *I navigate a fourteen-wheeler.* They warn, *Don't even bug me while I'm watching MTV.* They announce, *I'm going to the game; I'm coming from Wall Street;* and, *Where's the Empire State Building?* As a Capricorn, you want to make sure your clothes are not only speaking favorably of you, but are also keeping on track with your talking points, which include "I'm cool and in control; I'm a powerful player; respect me."

THREADS: The dressing rooms of life are full of people trying on stuff for all the wrong reasons—wearing trendy pieces that portray a whim or fantasy that hardly suits the woman underneath. You seldom fall for such fashion traps, as you're drawn to pieces that radiate classic style—the reliable, form-fitting cut of a certain designer; the blazer you can count on to look snazzy over an oxford shirt; or a drapey silk blouse that's sexy but still neat.

LUCKY FASHION PIECE: the pin-striped suit. It's as hardworking as you are—vest, jacket, pants, skirt, interchangeable all. Its professionalism is unmatched, while the playful pinstripes give overly serious the day off. Wearing the pinstripe, you remember your sense of humor while communicating the authority, competence, and esteem worthy of a promotion.

STYLE ESSENTIALS: a leather diary, an expensive pen, mysterious and austere designer sunglasses, shoes that look like you mean business, a watch that says, "I made it!"

STYLE EMBELLISHMENTS:

Scents: essence of bergamot or lemon oils.

Makeup: skincare. Cocoa butter and olive and sesame oils are très riche in antioxidants. Take care of your skin now, and it'll take care of you later.

Spa Splurges: Swedish Massage—shoulder stresses be gone!

HOW YOU EXPRESS YOURSELF: tactfully. Your clarity is sparkling, your exactness astounds. And since you're a public personality, it's necessary to demur from time to time. You believe revealing too much is a poor political move, and you may be right. Another inalienable right you possess: exercising your courage and grace, not for the meek of zodiac. Capricorn Marlene Dietrich said, "Courage and grace are a formidable mixture."

HOW YOU ROLL: The old adage "Dress for the job you want, not the job you have" applies just as aptly to your wheels. You select the car that would be appropriate for someone with the financial means you aspire to have. So what if your car payment is the same as your rent? More people see you in your car than will ever visit your house, so it's an expense that makes a difference. Of course, the ultimate luxury includes a car *and* a driver. From making phone calls to working on your laptop, you get so much accomplished during your commute that way.

GET YOUR PARTY ON: You make the appearance, put on a good face, and generally have a grand time. Maybe you have to go to the art opening; maybe you want to. What's the diff? Your social life always blurs into your professional life, making work a pleasure, and pleasure, work. You're an upwardly mobile goat, so you frequent places with purpose—say, where the elite meet to eat, the yacht club, or a hot new restaurant on opening night; in fact, you're probably a hidden investor.

CAPRICORN CELEBS GOT PERSONAL STYLE: Annie Lennox, Mary Tyler Moore, Bebe Neuwirth, Marlene Dietrich, Ava Gardner, Donna Summer, Diane Keaton, Joey Lauren Adams, Katie Couric, Pat Benatar, Naomi Judd.

★AQUARIUS★

AQUARIUS STYLE IN A WORD: forward.

IT'S ALL ABOUT THE: vision. You intuitively knew the trend was coming yesterday, so you wore it today, and surely they'll wear it tomorrow. Funny, you didn't intend to start a fashion revolution; it just happened to synergize with the way you live your life. After all, your style choices follow your life choices—maybe a piece is inspired by your latest spiritual studies, the new friend you just made, or that Himalayan trek you took. The best part of your easygoing approach to fashion is that living on the cutting edge makes you popular—and your standout friendliness makes you approachable, so others aren't afraid to ask, "Where did you find *that?*"

THREADS: Ecofashion fits you and your worldview perfectly. Clothes made from natural hemp fibers and dyes don't flatter everyone, nor do shoes designed from recycled rubber tires—but somehow you make them look so, well, cool. In fact, you make everything look cool by glamming it up. (Think the shearling-boot trend, a house slipper gone Hollywood.)

LUCKY FASHION PIECE: hip-hugger pants. Peace, love, and understanding, dude. As demonstrated through the ages by icons ranging from Mick Jagger to Britney Spears, low-slung pants are a hippie classic that encourage the wearer to wiggle, writhe, strut, dance, and be free. The belly-baring aspect of hip-huggers causes heated debates at many a PTA meeting, making it a favorite, albeit mild, teen rebellion.

Historical sidebar: Hip-huggers come into fashion when the world gets more chaotic. There's very convincing historical data that links waistline styles to oil prices: When one goes down, the other goes up.

STYLE ESSENTIALS FOR AQUARIUS: accessories for your accessories—such as cell phone charms, computer cases, changeable faces and cases for ipods and phones, dope sunglasses, a futuristic phone headset and other robotesque techno-gadgetry.

STYLE EMBELLISHMENTS:

Scent: Patchouli (not overdone) is your erotic musk.

Makeup: lip gloss.

Spa Splurges: Reiki Energy Treatment—you're the first to try it and the first to tell your friends, it actually works!

HOW YOU EXPRESS YOURSELF: honestly and from the hip. There's nothing wrong with the truth, Ruth. And even truth that would hurt coming from someone else will not hurt coming from you, because you're so light in your delivery that insults sound like quips, and rejections sound like kindness. As for formalities and written correspondence, they're not your favorite modes, as they require too much thought. You'd rather gush your thanks over the phone than express gratitude in a note—and you come off as so sincere that half the time no one even realizes that you didn't send a note.

HOW YOU ROLL: You never did understand the problem that other people seem to have with public transportation. It works beautifully in China and other countries that move with the masses, rather than the individual. It saves gas and it's good for the environment. A public bus, a VW bus, and a carshare with your friends all suit your liberated spirit equally.

GET YOUR PARTY ON: Charities, benefits, cause-worthy events—if there's a reason to get your party duds on, it's for a pleasure greater than your own. Where's Aquarian Oprah Winfrey tonight? Follow your favorite Aquarians to do-good events that celebrate the power of the human spirit to inspire, debate, help, and heal. Just be sure you bring your broad-minded, brainy friends along—to keep the conversation, and your interest, flowing with the champagne.

AQUARIUS CELEBS GOT PERSONAL STYLE: Oprah Winfrey, Sheryl Crow, Princess Caroline of Monaco, Bridget Fonda, Alicia Keys, Sarah McLach-

Ian, Minnie Driver, Lisa Marie Presley, Zsa Zsa Gabor, Lana Turner, Christina Ricci, Cybill Shepherd, Rene Russo.

★ PISCES ★

PISCES STYLE IN A WORD: ethereal.

IT'S ALL ABOUT THE: flow. Your approach to style is to honor the integrity of what is by not letting anything fight it. In clothing, this means keeping it simple and making sure that no item of clothing or accessory detracts from your overall look. Clothes that are fussy or require special care are usually more trouble than they're worth. The same goes for the rest of your belongings. The wise Pisces realizes that sooner or later, the things you own will own you. So in your view, the ultimate style statement uses minimal elements to make maximum, magical impact.

THREADS: Is it too much to ask that your clothing possess magical powers? Or at least, you'd like it to look like it does. If you could wear cobwebs to work, you would, because you feel divine in gossamer, dewy fabrics that give you the overall effect of floating. Your ideal wardrobe would be filled with pieces that move with a bit of magic and a just a smidgen of drama.

LUCKY FASHION PIECE: Fish can enjoy the sparkling shimmy of a sequined tank top. Fringes are fun, and so is a simple silver cami. It flirtatiously bounces your electric energy around the party, concert, or crowd.

STYLE ESSENTIALS: jewelry and stones that evoke a sacred feeling— religious and rock 'n' roll iconography, or shoes that look enchanted.

STYLE EMBELLISHMENTS:

Scents: lotus, sandalwood.

Makeup: shimmery eye shadow.

Spa Splurges: Reflexology—this foot treatment somehow calms your whole body and mind.

HOW YOU EXPRESS YOURSELF: telepathically. And when that doesn't work, poetic effusion is your second choice. For those who still can't seem to get the message through these methods, you find pleasure in articulating your emotions in that elegant, scrolling handwriting you've perfected.

HOW YOU ROLL: Your absolute favorite mode of transportation? That would be astral projection. Yeah, really. Wherever you go, you prefer that your mind goes first. The technique can be conscious, though you also tend to do it unconsciously. It goes like this: Say you have a business meeting tomorrow. You project yourself into that situation with as vivid a vision as possible, imagining yourself in the room, talking, laughing, and generally winning as you get down to biz with your associate. You picture the happy outcome. And you snap out of it, ready to have your actual meeting, which will probably happen more or less along the same lines.

GET YOUR PARTY ON: You can be quite impressionable, a quality that is especially apparent when you're in a celebratory situation. Your famous empathy can carry you to festive heights when you're in deliriously happy company, or to great depths when your guests are duds. That's why, when it's your turn to entertain, the guest list is the all-important party element to get right. You're fond of engineering seating charts, even for small groups, because you know you can orchestrate social brilliance by arranging your guests in surprising configurations.

PISCES CELEBS GOT PERSONAL STYLE: Cindy Crawford, Anaïs Nin, Nina Simone, Drew Barrymore, Erykah Badu, Elizabeth Taylor, Chelsea Clinton, Bernadette Peters, Juliette Binoche, Liza Minnelli, Queen Latifah, Glenn Close.

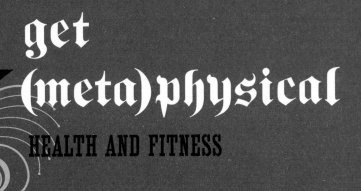

get (meta)physical

HEALTH AND FITNESS

Hey, sneezy, can't seem to kick that cold? Yo, lazy bones, still stuck on the sofa? Did you ever think that the remedy for what ails you, or the secret to achieving your highest level of vibrant vitality, may be . . . cosmic?

Don't be skeptical. History is full of bizarre, counterintuitive practices executed in the name of health and heartiness. For instance, bloodletting. "Yeah, she seems a little under the weather—maybe we should drain her life essence!" Or the pulling of wisdom teeth to ward off "bad humors"—in the days before anesthesia, no less. Yeesh.

Okay, so some of those so-called cures didn't turn out to be quite so appealing in the long run. But I'm talking about something far more organic, far more focused on working with your body than against it. And using astrology to help you get healthy—of body and mind—is a practice that has stood the test of time as an effective tool for centuries. It's the real deal.

In fact, health and wellbeing were one of the original applications of astrology. Medical texts have been discovered from the Hellenistic period associating body parts and organs with various degrees of the zodiac, and ailments and diseases have long been thought to be the fault of badly aspected planets. Saturn got blamed for breathing trouble, and Mars for fevers. But the planets were also considered to hold the cure: These same Hellenistic writings contained astrologically based remedies, such as medicinal plants that were picked and used according to the position of the sun and moon and their associations with the signs.

Hippocrates himself, the father of modern medicine, said that anyone who didn't use astrology in medicine was more of a clown than a doctor. Oh, those ancient Greeks—so extreme! So dramatic! But his point is a good one: The fusion of modern, Western medicine with a more spiritual, intuitive, worldly practice is what makes for a whole-body, whole-mind system of well-being. Not every cold needs a decongestant, and not every workout program requires a personal trainer. All you may need are your stars.

Good health is a blessing. It's also within your control. In fact, you are the only one in charge of your health—not your doctors, not your health insurance company (though it may seem otherwise after you've waited on hold for umpteen hours to get a referral for something you already know you need in the first place, thank you very much). So sit back and allow me to pour you a nice cool glass of cosmic consciousness, and read on about how you can use your planetary predilections to stay in shape.

Here's to your health!

★ ARIES ★

HOW ARIES STAYS FIT: When you apply your warrior spirit to a new fitness goal, you always wind up waving the victory flag. The headstrong ram is somewhat prone to headaches and head injuries, though, so be mindful of your mind container! Just wear the helmet and worry about your hair later. Staying hydrated is good preventative medicine for fire signs.

STAR HEALTH HABITS: So here's a star health habit for you: Where you go, so goes your bottle of water. And when it comes to nutrition, you'll find that apples and root vegetables like turnips, shallots, and yams pack a wallop of vitamins while keeping the calories compact—perfect for the lean, mean Aries machine.

FAB EXERCISE: spinning. Because Aries isn't sure she's exercised at all unless she leaves the gym drenched in sweat.

WORKOUT TIP: Just show up. Once you're in a place where workouts happen, they will.

GET SWEATY:

Favorite gear: Ten-speed bike—so you can go fast. Oh, and of course, don't forget your helmet. (Did I say that already?)

Best time: First thing in the morning.

Workout song: "Let's Get It Started," by the Black Eyed Peas.

★ 𝕿AURUS ★

HOW TAURUS STAYS FIT: The bull's tenacity often manifests itself physically as an almost freakish strength—wouldn't want to arm wrestle *you*. The body part associated with Taurus is the throat, which can be your power center or your most vulnerable spot. When stressed out, you're prone to sore throats, laryngitis, and coughs. That's why superior dental hygiene is so important for your sign—nix those bacteria before they get into your system.

STAR HEALTH HABITS: Protein-rich foods like seafood, eggs, beans, and rice are what your muscles need. But your heart has its own demands— chocolate, please. Go easy on those rich desserts, Taurus. Mini portions are your saving grace.

FAB TAURUS EXERCISE: hiking—or, as Taurus likes to call it, "being one with the earth."

WORKOUT TIP: You don't have to pay for your workout, but somehow it seems more fun when you do.

GET SWEATY:

Favorite gear: A personal trainer. You deserve it.
Best time: The morning after the steak dinner.
Workout song: "The Way You Love Me," by Faith Hill.

★ GEMINI ★

HOW GEMINI STAYS FIT: Your intellectual approach to health has you thinking ahead, practicing preventative medicine and backing your health-related decisions with research. Support your on-the-go lifestyle with several small meals a day, which keep you rocking at the high energy level you prefer.

STAR HEALTH HABITS: Sandwich bags filled with nutritious snacks act as secret weapons to ward off that bummer of a mood that comes when you're hungry. Legumes, nuts, honey, and citrus fruits are the lucky foods that help you avoid the bronchitis, colds, and allergies that can crop up when Gemini is feeling down. Plenty of sleep is also crucial for healthy Geminis, who may find the need to implement personal rules about caffeine consumption. My advice—respect the 4:00 PM cutoff point.

FAB EXERCISE: yoga, booty ballet, ball class—anything bouncy, trendy, and fun.

WORKOUT TIP: It's the daily things, like gardening, walking to a far-off parking place where you parked on purpose, or taking the stairs instead of the elevator, that make the biggest difference in your fitness level.

GET SWEATY:

Favorite gear: A DVD collection of fun workouts—lots of variety to keep you interested.

Best time: When the whim hits you.

Workout song: "Girl," by Beck.

★ CANCER ★

HOW CANCER STAYS FIT: With their holistic approach to health, Cancer girls figure out what's really going on so health problems can be not only fixed, but also prevented in the future. Being astutely aware of emotions that can make for more stress and anxiety-related ailments. Calcium-rich foods like yogurt and oysters help on a physical level, but humor and escapist vacations are what provide the mental break that sensitive souls like you need to restore your health to the fabulous zone.

STAR HEALTH HABITS: Ever equating food with motherly nurturing, Cancer girls find guilty pleasure in fresh-baked goods. It's also easy for the little crab to lose herself in a salty snack. Buying the prepackaged lunch-size portions can prevent the bloat that's found at the bottom of a twelve-ounce chip bag.

FAB EXERCISE: dancing, especially swing or ballroom, to simultaneously increase your passion and raise your heart rate.

WORKOUT TIP: Tell someone that you're going to work out. You'll wind up doing it just to stay honest.

GET SWEATY:

Favorite gear: a folding treadmill, so you can walk for miles in the perfectly temperate comfort of your own home.

Best time: When you get a mid-afternoon energy lull, exercise perks you up again.

Workout song: "Can't Fight the Moonlight," by LeAnn Rimes.

★ LEO ★

HOW LEO STAYS FIT: Save the money you were going to spend on vitamins, Leos. It's social conscience that keeps Leo girls healthy—the lion won't get sick if she thinks it will mean letting others down. Vanity is another quality that Leo can employ in the realm of health, because wanting to look good can be your best motivation for making healthy choices. Once Leo slips into mad-hot workout gear, the moves will follow.

STAR HEALTH HABITS: The predatory cat does love to indulge in decadence now and again and has nothing against adventurous choices, from moose steak to goose pâté. Lucky foods to help erase your culinary sins include eggplant, artichoke, sunflower seeds, and spinach.

FAB EXERCISE: jogging in a busy park (so lots of people will see the outfit).

WORKOUT TIP: Don't wing it. You're more secure when you have a plan. Preferably one that someone famous has followed.

GET SWEATY:

Favorite gear: A mirrored wall. It helps you maintain good form. Also, knowing what your whole body looks like in action motivates you toward your fitness goals.

Best time: When everyone else seems to be doing it.

Workout song: "Sunshine in the Shade," by the Fixx.

★ VIRGO ★

HOW VIRGO STAYS FIT: Virgos often look better at fifty than they do at twenty-five—a testament to a lifelong quest for perfect health. Your usual good habits are amplified by bouts of extreme self-care. In this mode, there is no part of your mind, body, or spirit that doesn't get lavished with loving attention. Spa services should be bought in bulk, right? If there's one thing you'd change about your constitution, it's the effect of nerves on your body. Alkaline foods such as artichoke, asparagus, broccoli, and kale help to restore your chemistry so you can think straight again.

STAR HEALTH HABITS: Virgos are the only sign that I feel compelled to caution against dieting. You tend to be too strict with yourself—and that, believe me, is worse than having the damn cream pie.

FAB EXERCISE: Pilates offers the graceful control you love to cultivate.

WORKOUT TIP: You don't have to have a perfect workout in order to get a benefit from it. Just do your best and be happy about what you did.

GET SWEATY:

Favorite gear: Paper towels. They are so versatile. Not only is cleaning at home a good workout, but you also use paper towels to wipe down whatever gear you're going to use at the gym, because, ewwwww!

Best time: Early in the morning. Get it out of the way.

Workout song: "Love Is in Control (Finger on the Trigger)," by Donna Summer.

★ LIBRA ★

HOW LIBRA STAYS FIT: Lucky for you, you're naturally attracted to things that are good for you, like brown rice and vegetables, long walks, massages, meditation, and taking life at an easy pace. Staying healthy is just a matter of honoring those proclivities. Reminding yourself constantly that you deserve perfect health is one habit that leads to a million small feel-good choices. Libra is associated with the lower back and holds stress in that area.

STAR HEALTH HABITS: Stretching is key for keeping that well-balanced bod moving in ways that others envy.

FAB EXERCISE: team sports (when teams are chosen, Libra is usually among the first picked), gymnastics, balancing yoga poses.

WORKOUT TIP: Buddy up. Even if you have to pay someone.

GET SWEATY:

Favorite gear: You can't possibly choose just one. That's what gym memberships are for.
Best time: When your workout partner is available.
Workout song: "Porcelain," by Moby.

★ SCORPIO ★

HOW SCORPIO STAYS FIT: For Scorpio, health is a matter of consciousness. Subconscious beliefs and stresses can be saboteurs (as anyone who has ever found herself "waking up" as her hand hits the bottom of the corn-chip sack can attest).

STAR HEALTH HABITS: Scorpio's healthiest habit is being willing to face what's really going down on deeper levels. Sure, you still love to get your party on, Scorpio—dine, dance, and flow the red, red wine. When you cross the lines of excess, tropical foods restore you—mango, coconut, even seaweed!

FAB EXERCISE: sexy stuff like belly dancing, pole dancing, and tango.

WORKOUT TIP: As a holistic being, you're better off focusing not on the results and measurements of fitness, but on how exercise makes you feel.

GET SWEATY:

Favorite gear: Ab strengtheners—grace comes from having a strong center.
Best time: Late. Long after the after-work crowd at the gym has gone home. You like as much privacy as possible.
Workout song: "Wake Me Up Inside," by Evanescence.

★ SAGITTARIUS ★

HOW SAGITTARIUS STAYS FIT: The secret equation for Sagittarian well-being is simple: Health equals optimism. There are many schools of medicine, but Western, Eastern, ayurvedic, and other practitioners agree that thinking happy thoughts is a powerful preventative potion.

Another key component to Sagittarian health is your spontaneity. You're always game for a round of tennis or catching a last-minute run around the park—anything to get the heart pumping.

STAR HEALTH HABITS: Sometimes you don't know when to call it quits. When excesses run you down, perk back up with raw salads, peppers, pears, beets, tomatoes, and lots of rest.

FAB EXERCISE: biking. Built for speed, you like exercise that gets the wind rushing in your face.

WORKOUT TIP: Get yourself a competitive partner. You're motivated to exercise when it's a game.

GET SWEATY:

Favorite gear: Heavy duty elastic bands—they function like free weights and you can pack them in a suitcase.

Best time: Any time, and all the time. It's like your whole life is a workout.

Workout song: "Bring Me Some Water," by Melissa Etheridge.

★ CAPRICORN ★

HOW CAPRICORN STAYS FIT: The billions of dollars spent annually on trendy diets, "miracle" beauty products, and quick-fix exercise gear are not, for the most part, coming from the pockets of Capricorn women. *Why do you need gear when you can open your front door and go for a jog?* thinks Capricorn. Still, it doesn't hurt to mix things up a bit. Stray from the basics. Try new foods a few times a month. Do the trendy exercise class just for the heck of it.

STAR HEALTH HABITS: You Capricorn women are known for your beautiful bone structure and gleaming, healthy teeth. But your real strength is your competitive edge. There's hardly a challenge you wouldn't jump at.

FAB EXERCISE: power-walking with an audio book—the perfect form of multitasking for your busy lifestyle.

WORKOUT TIP: Sometimes it feels like exercise is a luxury that you should save for after the "real work" is done. This couldn't be further from the truth! You can do more "real work" when your body is its healthiest!

GET SWEATY:

Favorite gear: Free weights—it's old school, and it works.

Best time: in the middle of the work day. It keeps you feeling energized way into overtime.

Workout song: "Sisters Are Doin' It for Themselves," by Annie Lennox.

★ AQUARIUS ★

HOW AQUARIUS STAYS FIT: Aquarius women enjoy impressively high metabolism and graceful physicality. You've been known to fly across a tennis court faster than a speeding bullet and leap over tall children in a single bound. The occasional sports injury (often affecting the shins or ankles) comes with the territory. But you Aquarians mend quickly, especially when you eat your lucky foods: watercress, celery, walnuts, peaches, and organic meat.

STAR HEALTH HABITS: It's not your first impulse to walk down the produce aisle—you have an occasional penchant for preservative-ridden snack foods with expiration dates in the next century. But eventually you always come back around to eating real food.

FAB EXERCISE: Themed aerobics classes with lots of moves to remember, like a hip-hop workout or chaos training, keep your mind as busy as your body is.

WORKOUT TIP: Bring your Bluetooth. You like to multitask by conversing through your fitness routine.

GET SWEATY:

Favorite gear: The elliptical machine appeal to your appreciation of beautifully executed and futuristic feeling design.

Best time: Mornings are for working out your brain, and evenings are for working out your bod.

Workout song: "Dreaming," by Blondie.

 ★ **PISCES** ★

HOW PISCES STAYS FIT: Adaptability. You realize that health is not dependent on a fixed system of rules but created on a day-to-day basis by meeting your current (and ever-changing) needs with the appropriate responses. Sunday it's leafy vegetables; Thursday it's pineapple.

STAR HEALTH HABITS: Tuning in to what your body is telling you is key. You don't find it the least bit weird that your body talks and you listen. Sometimes you even ask it questions out loud, such as, "Tummy, what would you like for breakfast?" or, "Legs, what kind of workout do you want today?" And your body's answer to such questions is far better than any outside advice.

FAB EXERCISE: swimming.

WORKOUT TIP: For you, the right music is everything.

GET SWEATY:

Favorite gear: Who needs gear when you've got two feet?

Best time: Sundown, so you can lavish in the sunset while you get your heart pumping—ah, heaven!

Workout song: "New Shoes," by Paolo Nutini.

★ ACKNOWLEDGMENTS ★

THANK YOU TO Laura Mazer, the Virgo-licious champion of this project without whom it would not be. Thank you for the brilliant and tireless work of Annie Tucker, Darcy Cohan, and Domini Dragoone.

Thank you to the paternal trinity, Leonard Hebert, Roger Jacks, and Larry Mathis, and to all my fab family.

Thank you to the Astro-Girl Sign Study Posse: Amy Gibbons, Amy Shrekengaust, Ana Jardines, April Hebert, Belinda Cassas-Welles, Cara Peters, Christiane Schul, Cindy Bottomley, Claudia Hoover, Daisy Adams, Emelia Barnum, Erica Camp, Glenda Cates, Irene Biery, Jackie Holroyd, Janet

Eargle, Jenna Poinier, Joy Brough, Kathryn Schorr, Laura Schiff, Lexi Ridaught, Ma Ananda Shreemati, Maria Peters, Melissa Eltringham, Michelle Vick, Mini Carlsson, Rae Dawn Hattinger, Shawn Isbell, Stephanie Harpel, Susan Thiele, Tracy Rane, Vicky Curtis, the Bullards and the Jays.

A special thanks to: Billie Nordahl, Vylna Mathis, James and Gloria Cates, Shannon Burwell, Laura Manske, Mara Brown, Bernie Barlow, Jeannie Lurie, Kelly Moneymaker, Jill Spiegel, Jessica Shepherd, Michael Brooks, Dilana Robichaux, Michael Levin, Jim, Jeff, Jeffrey and Greg Cates, Thane Mathis, Kathy Kei, the Creators Crew, Joe Curtis, Joe Gallagher, Jay Tinsky, Peter Reckell, Gahl Sasson, Rich Roll, Bob Hebert, Rick Newcombe and Cathy Hurst.

Thank you, loyal astrology readers!

Thank you to the bright spirit of Joyce Jillson.

★ ABOUT THE AUTHOR ★

© STUART MATHIS

HOLIDAY MATHIS apprenticed with celebrity astrologer Joyce Jillson for more than a decade before she began writing her own horoscope column. She became known as "the Rock 'n' Roll Astrologer" by predicting hot CD release dates and fortuitous artist/producer combinations for some of the biggest artists on the Billboard charts.

In addition to being a newspaper columnist, Holiday is also an author and a triple-platinum-selling songwriter. She has published three children's books, and her award-winning songs have been featured in films and on television, including *Agent Cody Banks, Desperate Housewives, South of Nowhere, Hannah Montana,* and *Unfabulous,* and on albums by young pop stars Emma Roberts, Miley Cyrus, and Katy Rose.

Holiday's horoscope column is distributed by Creators Syndicate, and it appears in more than 300 newspapers worldwide. She also writes for *Quick & Simple* magazine. Holiday lives in Southern California with her daughter and husband, Stuart Mathis, a lead guitarist and songwriter who has recorded and toured with The Wallflowers, Jewel, Lifehouse, Five for Fighting, Lisa Marie Presley, Missy Higgins, Chris Isaak, LeAnn Rimes, and others.

Holiday can be found at www.rockyourstars.com.

SELECTED TITLES FROM SEAL PRESS

For more than thirty years, Seal Press has published groundbreaking books. By women. For women. Visit our website at www.sealpress.com.

The Anti 9-to-5 Guide: Practical Career Advice for Women Who Think Outside the Cube by Michelle Goodman. $14.95, 1-58005-186-3. Escape the wage-slave trap of your cubicle with Goodman's hip career advice on creating your dream job and navigating the work world without compromising your aspirations.

It's So You: 35 Women Write About Personal Expression Through Fashion and Style edited by Michelle Tea. $15.95, 1-58005-215-0. From the haute couture houses of the ruling class to DIY girls who create their own hodgepodge style, this is the first book to explore women's ambivalence toward, suspicion of, indulgence in, and love of fashion on every level.

Offbeat Bride: Taffeta-Free Alternatives for Independent Brides by Ariel Meadow Stallings. $15.95, 1-58005-180-4. Part memoir and part anecdotal how-to, *Offbeat Bride* is filled with sanity-saving tips, advice, and stories to guide even the most out-there bride.

Woman's Best Friend: Women Writers on the Dogs in Their Lives edited by Megan McMorris. $14.95, 1-58005-163-4. An offbeat and poignant collection about those four-legged friends girls can't do without.

Cinderella's Big Score: Women of the Punk and Indie Underground by Maria Raha. $17.95, 1-58005-116-2. A tribute to the transgressive women of the underground music scene, who not only rocked as hard as the boys, but also tested the limits of what is culturally acceptable—even in the anarchic world of punk.

Chick Flick Road Kill: A Behind-the-Scenes Odyssey into Movie-Made America by Alicia Rebensdorf. $15.95, 1-58005-194-4. A twentysomething's love-hate relationship with picture-perfect Hollywood sends her on a road trip in search of a more real America.